PRAISE FOR THE PERSONAL AGII

"This book transcends any category of business or self-development genre today. It encompasses the full lifecycle of actionable thought leadership to ensure you can align personal and professional goals. I recommend other CEOs do Personal Agility with their executive team."
— **Ben Sever, CEO**
   eRemede

"Personal Agility enabled us to create transparency and alignment among the Board members and Chief Officers. We agreed on What Really Matters moving forward. As it became clear what we needed to do, we could all agree both on what and why, so we could move forward without resistance or hesitation."
— **Michael Mrochen, Chairman of the Board**
   Vivior AG

"The true genius of Personal Agility is how simple it is to implement. Personal Agility gives you the compass that can help you get things done that matter. The tools and techniques made me a better coach. Personal Agility is a hidden gem!"
— **Jim Hannon EdD, Founder**
   Boston University Agile Innovation Lab

"Thanks to Personal Agility, I can finish each week with satisfaction and start each week with confidence."
— **Walter Stulzer, Executive Director**
   Futureworks AG

"This system gives you the means to create clarity and focus."
— **Michael K Sahota**
   Leading Beyond Change

"Maria Matarelli and Peter Stevens have connected the Agile principles and values that help teams wildly succeed to something far more personal, more human."
— **Howard Sublett, CEO**
   Scrum Alliance

"PAS will help you cut through the noise. It will guide you to identify What Really Matters, then on making progress every day on the most important things. You'll be shocked by how much more you achieve, with more free time and less stress.
— **Karim Harbott**
The 6 Enablers of Business Agility

"The Personal Agility System has not only helped me focus on building my business but played a vast role in shaping my life as a striving entrepreneur. It became a way of life and brought tremendous transformations that are clearly measurable!"
— **Dhanushka Arjuna, Founder**
ZeroBelow, Germany

"Personal Agility is something we all may think we don't need, but it's the most important thing missing in our lives."
— **Satyajit Nath, Director**
Hyderabad, India

"The Personal Agility Questions were a helpful refactor in my own reflective practice. Personal Agility is about intentionally choosing and acting on the most important areas to make the biggest impact with the most rewarding return."
— **Pete Behrens, Founder**
Agile Leadership Journey

"As the world continues to change at a rapid pace and uncertainty abounds, Personal Agility equips professionals with tools, thinking and practical examples necessary to know how to thrive. This highly enjoyable book is your guide from chaos to clarity.
— **Jorgen Hesselberg, Co-Founder**
Comparative Agility

"Personal Agility enabled me to feel more in control of my life. My goals became more achievable, and I found purpose and happiness"
— **Adelina Stefan, ICF Professional Certified Coach**
Switzerland

PERSONAL AGILITY

Unlocking **PURPOSE, ALIGNMENT** and **TRANSFORMATION**

PETER B. STEVENS & MARIA MATARELLI

To request permissions, contact the publisher
at books@businessagility.institute

First paperback edition September 2022. Version 9.13.

Edited by Christopher Ruz
Book design by Sinisa Poznanovic
Layout by QLEVIO

ISBN: 978-1-957600-19-2 (Hardcover)
ISBN: 978-1-957600-15-4 (Paperback)
ISBN: 978-1-957600-18-5 (Digital)

Reprinted by permission.

Published by Business Agility Institute, LLC
https://businessagility.institute

an imprint of
QLEVIO
BAI press

To contact the authors, visit:

Personal Agility Institute LLC
https://personalagilityinstitute.org

ACKNOWLEDGEMENTS

The essence of Agility includes collaboration and learning from each other. This has enabled both the Personal Agility System (PAS) and this book to become what they are today. Along our journey, we have worked with many individuals and organizations whom we would like to thank here:

- The early contributors, especially Kamila Duniec and John Socha, who helped unearth the What Really Matters question.

- Lyssa Adkins, Alistair Cockburn, and Joe Justice for giving us encouragement and validating our understanding of agility and professional coaching.

- The Personal Agility Recognized Ambassador (PARA) community: Amogh Sukhatankar, Fadly Arisandy Rasyad, Ilham N Musayev, Ipsita Mishra, Jan Farkas, Jatin Sanghavi, Johanna Hurtado Morales, Katrina Snow, Nagini Chandramouli, Pete Blum, Pierre Neis, Sakthi Chandrasekar, Satyajit Nath, Senela Jayasuriya, Sharon Geurin, Shikha Kathuria, Sriram Rajagopalan, Susannah Chambers, Tobias Glaser, and Yaara Kaminer.

- Within the PARA community, a special thanks to Shweta Jaiswal, Piyali Karmakar, Janani Liyanage, Adelina Stefan, Jyoti Dandona, Liviu Mesesan, Jim Hannon, Hugo Lourenco, and Gail Ferreira, who, as passionate early adopters, helped advance and define Personal Agility, both as movement and a school of thought.

- Our clients who volunteered to share their stories as case studies, including Michael Mrochen, Ben Sever, Walter Stulzer, Jörg Ewald, Larry Pakeiser, Andreas Kelch, Katrina Snow, Pete Blum, Sara A., Gabriel Chiriac, Adriana Carrano, José Albuquerque, Karina Schneider, Cory Schroeder, Tuhan Sapumange, and most especially, Sharon Geurin who inspired us with her story to document the success of PAS with case studies.People around the world who have chosen to become Personal Agility Recognized Practitioners (PARPs). As early adopters, you have trusted us and helped us to develop both PAS as a framework and our approach to teaching and sharing Personal Agility.

- The experts we met on the Marketing Cruise 2017, especially Iman Aghay and George Verdolaga. Imagine an Open Space conference on a Caribbean cruise ship. There is a reason we talk about "Jamaica" in our metaphors.

- Peter's friends in the "Pizza call" (we don't actually eat pizza during the pizza call) who have been sources of advice, challenge, and inspiration: Andrew Holm, Dawna Jones, Jay Goldstein, Stephen Denning, Dr. Thomas Juli, John Styffe, and Nancy Van Schooenderwoert.

- The World Agility Forum, held annually in Lisbon, Portugal, for recognizing leaders and organizations for their outstanding application of Personal Agility, and for hosting the Executive Roundtable on Personal Agility at eXperience Agile and Agile Human Factors. Special thanks to Hugo Lourenco and Paula Magalhaes and their team that hosts these annual events.

- Jim Hannon and the Boston University Agile Innovation Lab for developing a program with the Personal Agility System for graduate students.

- Jorgen Hesselberg and the team at Comparative Agility for recognizing Personal Agility as a powerful capability on their Agility assessment and continuous improvement platform.

- The Scrum Alliance for recognizing our work and publishing our interviews and articles on Agility beyond software.

- The Agile community around the world for giving us the opportunity to speak and share about Personal Agility at their conferences, meetups, and podcasts.

- Rene Wettler, Pino Decandia, Rijon Erickson, Katharina Knoche, Bertrand Jakob, Christine Schmucki and Dhanushka Arjuna for additional support and inspiration. And a special thank you to everyone else who believes in our mission!

- Our publisher, the Business Agility Institute, in particular Evan Leybourn and our amazing editor, Chris Ruz, for helping to finalize the book and bring it to the world.

- Sabine Stevens, who put the celebrate into Celebrate and Choose.

We'd like to express a special thank-you to the those who sponsored our work and by doing so supported us above and beyond the call of duty: Alex Sidorecs, Ash Tiwari, Bernard Boodeea Herbert Segura, Jane Noesgaard Larsen, Johanna Hurtado

Morales, John Farrow, Kiro Harada, Magdalena Gałaj, Marcus Ward, Nancy Endrizzi, Raymond Cheong, and Sebastian Sussmann.

TABLE OF CONTENTS

FOREWORD
by Alistair Cockburn

Over the last 30 years, I have seen overworked employees, their overworked bosses, and solo entrepreneurs burning themselves out. The syndrome of running as fast as you can just to keep from going backwards is found all across the world. This book helps with that.

When you run hard, you should advance. For all your work, you should find joy. Peter Stevens and Maria Matarelli have written a marvelous little book that will help you do both. It's easy to read and contains questions, reflections, insights, tips, and techniques that will help you recenter your life and progress toward your goals.

They demonstrate how you can use their reflective tools in your personal life, in reaching your personally stated professional goals, and in your corporate professional activities, if you have those.

This book contains personal stories of people I know, people whom I have seen change their lives. I have seen Maria herself use these tools to achieve her remarkable current careers (plural, yes!—she even became an international DJ!).

Personal Agility is more than just completing your tasks more efficiently. It is about selecting the path that speaks to your heart and moving along that path using the same or less energy than you were burning before. Read the stories, learn the simple, reflective techniques, and see for yourself. Happy travels.

FOREWORD
by Lyssa Adkins

I have been an Agilist for 15 years and have been applying Agile in my personal life for a long time (just ask my family about the sticky notes on the kitchen cabinets). The Personal Agility System has taken this to a new level. The coaching questions led me to really look at how I spend my time and whether I am honoring What Really Matters to me. It's forced me to face some hard choices, but the process was worth it because I have gained powerful alignment with my business and life mission. I also experience joy knowing I am doing more of what energizes me while also fulfilling that mission.

When you are in the habit of always doing more and more without stopping to celebrate your achievements, the pattern of saying "yes" when you know your plate is full becomes an occupational hazard.

The secret never told is there is a dependency, even a sort of addiction to performing at a high level and moving from one challenge to the next with barely a breath in between. It overwhelms you and before you know it, things that matter most start to slip away.

It took me a while to consistently direct my attention to what should've been at the top of my priorities list all along, including rest and rejuvenation. I had to shift my belief about success requiring that I be "always on" and, instead, come to the realization that rest and rejuvenation *are* an essential part of the work. PAS helped me re-wire this belief and create the habits that sustained it.

In this book you will find the roadmap you need to break through whatever limiting beliefs you currently hold, while creating structure and alignment so you can achieve greatness in the areas that matter most to you.

While working with Maria Matarelli and the Personal Agility Institute, I have loved being involved with groups going through the process.

I love hearing stories from people pulling themselves out of desperate financial situations, losing weight, landing a job that is worthy of them, rescuing their struggling business or saving relationships.

What I've learned is that everyone does it a little bit differently, but the results are the same: a more conscious way of living and achieving that brings results while also providing genuine fulfillment and balance. PAS helps me stay true to what matters most to me in my whole life: my work life, my long-term vision, my personal life... all of it. I have had so many *ah-ha's* during this time, and I have come to understand Agile on a much deeper level. I've even coached Agile teams to help them really "get" these lessons. But I've never been on an Agile team as a team member, so I hadn't experienced them myself.

Studying Personal Agility unlocked a whole new depth of Agile for me to integrate. I can now say that, because of my experience using Personal Agility, I can now grok so many of the lessons of Agile bone deep because I have had a direct, lived experience of them. They are not simply concepts; they are visceral learnings. I believe PAS is a powerful way for organizational leaders, who will never be on an Agile team, to have the same experience I did and to be able to integrate these lessons directly so that Agility can flourish in their organizations and in their own lives.

FOREWORD

by Stephen Denning

When Satya Nadella took over as CEO of Microsoft in 2014, many critics thought that the firm was on its last legs. Microsoft's software products were in decline. Its old, static products lacked pizzazz and personified "boring." Its investment in the Nokia phone was disastrous. All the places in Big Tech were taken. Google owned search. Facebook owned social. Apple owned communications. Microsoft's revenues were flat and its share price was stagnant. Staff were demoralized and few saw a viable path forward. Microsoft seemed to be a relic of an industrial-era company that, like so many other big firms, had failed to grasp and master the meaning of the emerging digital economy.

Most firms undertaking a digital transformation soldier on with their losing, industrial-era business models while they dabble in digital innovation on the side. The common result: the loss of energy that is sucked into the losing business models prevents the firm from ever putting its heart into digital innovation. The firm muddles along, cutting costs to make money, as the stock market punishes its lackluster performance and lack of growth prospects. In due course, the firm's board loses patience, and a new CEO is hired to restart the cycle.

But Nadella had different ideas. One of the first things he did was to signal what Microsoft would not do. He did the unthinkable and announced that the firm would no longer pursue its flagship product, Windows, as a business. He also announced that Microsoft would no longer pursue the Nokia phone despite the sunk cost.

Instead, Microsoft would devote its efforts to things where it could make a difference. These decisions freed up time and energy to pursue more promising avenues. Seven years later, with a two-trillion-dollar increase in Microsoft's market capitalization, the critics were shown to be wrong. Microsoft not only had a future: it was now one of the richest and fastest-growing firms in the world. To accomplish this, Nadella had to do a number of things right, but the most important of those was to do what new CEOs rarely do: say what he would not do.

The late professor of anthropology at the London School of Economics, David Graeber, wrote eloquently about the problem of useless work being done in organizations. The workplace, he found, was riddled with work that was so completely pointless, unnecessary, or pernicious that even the employee could not justify its existence even though, as part of the conditions of employment, the employee feels obliged to pretend that this is not the case. He conducted surveys that showed that the amount of unnecessary work being done in large firms was over 40% of the total work being performed—work to which someone should have said no.

The primary responsibility for creating and maintaining pointless work obviously rests with managers, but workers themselves are increasingly taking matters into their own hands. In 2021, the COVID-19 pandemic caused many workers to rethink their careers, work conditions, and long-term goals. As many workplaces attempted to bring their employees back in-person, an astonished number of workers declined. With telecommuting also came schedule flexibility, and many workers (particularly in younger cohorts) sought to gain a better work–life balance.

Personal Agility by Peter B. Stevens and Maria Matarelli creates a framework for deciding when and why to say no. The key question is, "What Really Matters?" Personal Agility provides a pathway for deciding how to live a meaningful, purpose-driven life. It generates a way of stepping back from the hustle and bustle of the day-to-day grind and thinking about whether you're doing the right things. It points the way towards waking up every morning excited and ending every day fulfilled—in other words, aligned with both the people around you and what is most important in your life. It helps create the results you want in your life and at work.

Personal Agility starts from the premise that time is your most valuable currency. It's a resource you only get to spend once. The book enables you to think systematically about how much of your time you're spending on things that really matter.

It shows how great things can happen when you align what you do with What Really Matters. It provides documented stories of people who have completely changed the direction of their lives, both in stopping doing unproductive things and in committing to new endeavors and new relationships.

Personal Agility is a book to study and learn from. You might think of it as a guidebook to life.

INTRODUCTION

> *"Agility is for executives, and we have the data to prove it."*
>
> **Nayomi Handunnetti,**
> **Executive Director of Handun Villas**
> **and Restaurants, Colombo, Sri Lanka**

Walter Stulzer had a problem. He was the executive director of Future-works, a creative consultancy in Zurich he'd spun off from a larger consultancy two years previously. But the new company wasn't profitable.

For two years he tried traditional approaches to address the problem. They defined measures, but there were too many initiatives, which left his staff scrambling to do too many things at once without getting any of them done. He also had serious issues with staff turnover.

The situation was getting critical. "We had liquidity problems," Walter said. "That is, we were close to having no money in the bank account. We were about to run into a wall. Without a rapid improvement, bankruptcy was inevitable. I needed to make changes fast to save the company."

Walter began using Personal Agility as a new approach. "This allowed us to focus on the essentials and make educated guesses on what to do next. With each step, we would learn and inspect and adapt. Even if what we did was the wrong thing, we could learn quickly, and the damage from one misstep was limited. We could reorder, reprioritize, and make better guesses the next time."

Personal Agility gave Walter and his company a new approach and helped them focus on the essentials, achieving in six months what they had previously failed to do in two years. In other words: they hit all their goals with half the work in a quarter of the time.

For Walter, the bottom line was clear: "I can now end each day with satisfaction and start each day with confidence."

Waking with confidence and ending the working day satisfied is a dream many of us share. Whether you're a business owner or employee, entrepreneur or contractor, stay-at-home spouse or caregiver, freelancer, or CEO, you likely relate to the idea of being able to focus on the essentials, adapt to unforeseen challenges and situations, and being able to go to bed at night knowing you've made measurable strides towards success.

Personal Agility can be the path that guides you to that success. It is a system of self-management and self-reflection that helps you identify What Really Matters to you, create measurable and concrete steps towards achieving your goals, and tracking the steps you take to maintain your energy and momentum along the journey.

While Personal Agility is built upon the foundations of Business Agility and borrows from its principles and processes, it is not limited to the workplace. The lessons you will learn throughout this book can be equally applied to the founding of a business or the renovation of your home, the transformation of an IT team or your quest to complete your university degree.

You're likely already aware of how quickly local and international markets are changing, and how technological advancements are disrupting entire industries. Many brands and even industries from just a few decades ago no longer exist. Exponential product and performance improvements combined with a convergence of new technologies means that businesses must innovate better than ever before. Like Walter, many corporate leaders are turning to Agility to help them face these challenges.

Whether you're a seasoned Business Agility veteran or someone for whom these concepts are entirely new, this book will provide you with the foundations you need to get through those changes and disruptions by making your ways of working more flexible and adaptable.

> *"Exponential changes and the convergence of technologies are driving the world to change completely. If you are not riding the wave, you are toast."*
>
> **Vivek Wadhwa,**
> **speaking at the World Agility Forum,**
> **Lisbon, Portugal**

In business, *silos* refer to teams, departments, or individuals that work entirely separated from their colleagues, without sharing resources, information, or talent. Today, companies need to work not only across silos in their organizations, but across industries and technologies to leverage their potential. The companies who can't do this will be "toast": bankrupt, forgotten, or irrelevant.

Just as Personal Agility gives individuals the tools they need to solve personal problems, it also gives business leaders the tools they need to solve problems, achieve goals, and guide and prioritize collaboration. You can create alignment between what you do and What Really Matters while building alignment among stakeholders and customers. This enables both decisiveness and focus.

If 20th century leadership was about managing the machine to produce profits reliably, the 21st is about innovation in the face of complexity and uncertainty. Leaders need new skills to activate the intelligence of their workforces and enable collaboration across boundaries, both internal and external.

Modern leadership is as much about culture as it is about goals. Culture is about people and the interactions between them. The challenge starts in the head and the heart of each individual. The Personal Agility System (PAS) offers a scalable approach to leadership that can enable organizations, departments, teams, and even couples and individuals, to align what they do with What Really Matters.

Personal Agility gives your teams and departments the tools and perspective they need to work together in alignment with the needs of your customers and the goals of the organization. Your people can collaborate more effectively, across departments or even organizations, to satisfy your customers, create new market needs and then fulfill them. You can have confidence that people are working together, effectively and on the right things.

Imagine waking up every morning excited and ending each day feeling fulfilled; Feeling in alignment with the people around you and what is most important in your life, vibrant and happy, living in flow, fulfilling your life's purpose. Creating the results you want in your life and at work.

Sharon Guerin inspired us to begin documenting what people could accomplish through Personal Agility. Sharon, a single mother, was barely getting by while working five jobs. By applying PAS, and with a little help from her coach and mentor, she became a successful entrepreneur with a six-figure income in her first year of business. She took it to the next level by landing a six-figure client the following year and then went on to apply PAS to lose more than 55 lbs. (25kg) and greatly improve her health and quality of life.

Our case studies document how people have achieved dramatic, measurable results by applying PAS. Walter's company rebounded from near bankruptcy to profitability. Another company improved their on-time project completion rate from 24% to over 75%. An early-stage start-up completed their three-year roadmap and achieved their target $35 million dollar valuation in just 18 months.

People from around the world and from all walks of life are applying PAS to address their challenges and achieve their goals. In these pages, you will follow the stories of men, women, CEOs, entrepreneurs, students and more as they apply PAS to figure out What Really Matters, do what they need and want to do, and overcome obstacles to achieve their goals and become who they want to be.

The Personal Agility System invites you to live with intention, meaning, and fulfillment to create a better life. This invitation extends to your professional life, where you can achieve greater success for yourself and your organization.

For us, the most dramatic learning came as we realized the long-term impact our approach could have and how broadly PAS could be applied. Sharon was our first case study. After hearing her story, we did the research and concluded that there are probably 100 million people like Sharon in the United States alone, all struggling to get by. What if we could enable just 1% of them to transform their lives like she did? What if we could help leaders get incredible results in business like Walter?

This book reaches the heart of humanizing business by providing a simple framework for individual and business transformation. It explains how to apply Agility to any context and documents the positive transformations that can be achieved. We share real case studies about results that people and organizations have achieved by applying PAS.

This book is divided into two parts. The first part covers the basics of leading yourself. You will discover the navigation metaphor, six powerful questions, and tools for visualizing your course and position.

From the first chapter, you'll be able to figure out What Really Matters to you or your project. Soon, you will be able to recognize and react to distractions and procrastination to achieve long-term goals effectively.

We introduce a powerful metaphor for achieving long term-goals based on the concept of navigating the ocean to a faraway destination. If, say, Jamaica represents your goal, then the winds, waves and storms represent the urgent interruptions and distractions of daily life. You are the captain of your ship and Personal Agility is your GPS Navigator that helps you find your way through all that complexity to your personal Jamaica.

The second part extends Personal Agility from leading yourself to leading others. We introduce you to dialogue, a fundamental skill that enables you to lead through empowerment. You will learn how to apply the techniques of Personal Agility at work to solve problems, create alignment, agree on direction, take decisions, and hold focus. You get tools to strengthen your relations with your customers, board members, and other stakeholders. You can create a more responsive organization.

By the time you finish the book, you'll be able to scale your leadership skills from the personal to the organizational. You will have tools to achieve understanding and alignment with the people around you, and you will be able to forge a shared vision and achieve it together.

Where is your destination? Would you like to go there? Let's get started.

PART ONE:
LEADING YOURSELF

Once upon a time, the world seemed much simpler than it is today.

These days, there is so much to do and not enough time to do it. Getting things done is only part of the problem. The bigger challenge is handling the endless flood of demands coming from life, work, social media, and more.

In this section, you will learn how to create alignment with yourself, so you can figure out What Really Matters and spend more of your time on these things. You will then learn how to achieve your goals while dealing with procrastination, distractions, and other challenges of daily life and work.

If you have a dream, Personal Agility can help you achieve it. PAS has already transformed many lives and could do so for millions more. We will share several compelling case studies to highlight what's possible.

In business, the software industry was among the first to be confronted with the complexities of the modern world. In 2001, a group of software developers published the Agile Manifesto. This launched the Agile movement which revolutionized product development and is now expanding to include leadership and nearly every other function in an organization.

The first element of the Agile Manifesto was about the importance of individuals and the interactions between them.

Your journey to achieve your goals starts with you as an individual.

CHAPTER 1.
SIX QUESTIONS TO CHANGE YOUR LIFE

In this chapter, you will learn about the fundamentals of Personal Agility. You will begin by exploring and internalizing the guiding principle of identifying What Really Matters. Next, you'll learn about how life is an ocean and how Personal Agility can help you navigate across it. After that, you'll dive deep into Six Powerful Questions that you'll use throughout every step of your Personal Agility Journey.

With the Six Questions in hand, you'll be ready to explore the differences between Leading Yourself and Leading Others. You'll also learn about the five key elements that define Personal Agility, and how it differs and goes beyond other methods of improving personal productivity. Finally, with all these concepts in hand, you'll explore how to use this book to improve your day-to-day life, your business, your relationships, and more.

> *"It's not that we don't have enough time.*
> *We have too much to do."*
>
> **Kent Beck**

Hugo Lourenco is an entrepreneur based in Lisbon, Portugal, who owns a consultancy and several other businesses. He wanted to kick off a new generation of products and services for his customers.

"I was working like crazy, but not getting a valuable return on the time that I was investing. I found myself working with seven organizations and I was too busy working to achieve my long-term goals. The problem was that I had to recover from a previous business failure, support my family and reinvent the business. I felt a strong need to accept every paying gig I was offered, regardless of whether it was profitable or serving my long-term interests. I couldn't bring myself to say 'no'."

Hugo knew he needed greater control over his life, as he was constantly working and not really enjoying it. He needed to be able to say 'no' despite the risks involved, so he could focus more and be successful.

"I started saying 'no', to myself first, then politely getting myself away from those activities that consumed so much time without bringing any joy. I have more perspective and can make better decisions. I am working smarter, not harder."

Today, in addition to running his businesses, Hugo is the President of the World Agility Forum and the eXperience Agile Conference, two of the most prestigious global conferences in Europe.

"What Really Matters (WRM) played a key role. If I know why I am doing it, I can justify it—even if there are risks involved. Today, I use the PAS Priorities Map every day, as does our staff, so that we all stay focused on What Really Matters."

Time is your most valuable currency. You only get to spend it once. Your health is your most valuable asset. If you lose it, you may never find it again. How much of your time are you spending on things that really matter? Do you have too much to do and not enough time to do it?

PAS is a simple framework that helps you align what you do with What Really Matters. At the heart of Personal Agility are Six Powerful Questions to help you visualize and reflect on what you are doing so you can choose the actions that will help you achieve the results you want.

With Personal Agility, you create a radar screen that enables you to see and evaluate the forces that push and pull you through life. You can choose the activities that get you where you want to go.

Achieving long term goals requires perseverance and awareness. PAS introduces a navigation metaphor for understanding where you are and where you are going. It is a GPS for your life to help you recognize when you are drifting off course so you can correct where you are heading.

The same skills that enable you to align what you do with what you care about also enable you to build a common understanding with the people around you regarding What Really Matters, be they family at home or stakeholders at work. This in turn enables true alignment. You become trustworthy, a problem solver, and a leader.

When you align what you do with What Really Matters at work, even more great things happen. Alignment is the holy grail of business. Less than 10% of all organizations successfully execute their strategies due to lack of alignment.[1] When people are aligned, they solve problems together rather than fight over whose solution is the right solution. Work becomes fun and pointless conflict disappears, especially in leadership teams.

How do you know if you are on course to achieve your goals? First, let's explore the navigation metaphor; then you can apply this concept to sailing toward your long-term goals while dealing with the storms of interruptions, distraction, and procrastination along the way.

I. NAVIGATION METAPHOR: LIFE IS THE OCEAN

Imagine you're on a sailing ship in the ocean. Where is that ship? Well, that's kind of hard to tell. You need some tools for navigation. Traditionally, this would include a clock and sextant, which fixed your position by measuring the sun and the stars. Today, you would use a Global Positioning System (GPS) Navigator.

Where is the ship headed? That depends. If the ship has no captain, no drive, and no rudder, then the ship will be taken somewhere by the wind, the waves, and the currents. A GPS navigator can tell you where you are, and based on where you've been, can predict where the ship is heading.

Where will the ship arrive and when? That's hard to tell too. The course can change with every fluctuation in the weather. Winds can blow the ship aground, or the waves and storms could tear the boat apart. Without the wind or an engine to drive the ship forward, and without a captain to set the destination and hold the course, that ship could end up anywhere or drift for a long time in the middle of the ocean.

The GPS can tell you where you are and confirm that you are on course. If you drift off course, the GPS can suggest course corrections to get you back on track.

---

[1] Larry Myer, Forbes Contributor, Strategy 101: *It's All About Alignment.* https://www.forbes.com/sites/larrymyler/2012/10/16/strategy-101-its-all-about-alignment/

If life is an ocean, then you are the captain of your ship. How do you get to your destination? Let's say you're heading to Jamaica. The winds, waves and currents represent the conflicting forces in your life. Most of them won't take you to Jamaica. You bring the drive and choose the destination. Add the ability to know where you are and where you are going, and you can set and hold your course.

Think of Personal Agility as a GPS Navigator for your life. Jamaica represents your goal or destination, i.e., the deeper why. What Really Matters represents your navigation stars that keep you on course to your destination.

You are who you are because you do what you do. The decisions you make about what to do reflect What Really Matters to you. They also reveal your course (or lack of one). By changing what you do, you can change who you are.

If you are not in alignment with yourself or if what you do does not reflect the person you want to be, you are less likely to be happy, satisfied, or feel fulfilled. By adjusting your priorities, by doing more things that matter, you can change your course to become the person you want to be and accomplish the things you want most.

What happens if you get caught in a storm? The seas are rough! The waves are crashing over the railings! You can't see the stars to navigate, and even if you could, you don't have time. The ship could sink! You are the captain — what is your job?

- Don't let the ship sink.
- When the seas calm down, determine your location and resume navigating to your destination.

Sometimes there are stormy seasons, and it's okay just to maintain and keep the ship afloat. Storms can be intense, on the ocean and in your life. If your ship is still afloat, then you're still in the game, and every arcade gamer knows that "game over" is just an invitation to put another coin in the slot and play again.

So even if most of your time is spent doing things you feel you absolutely have to do, you are still the captain of your life. At any point, you can stop and reflect and ask yourself if there is anything you'd like to change. You can set aside some time each week—even if it's just an hour—working toward a better future and better you.

II. SIX POWERFUL QUESTIONS

If time is your most valuable currency, then how you want to spend it, how you ought to spend it, and how you do spend it all give insight into What Really Matters to you. When these three aspects agree, then you are in alignment with yourself. When there are significant differences between them, this is a sign that you are drifting off course.

It's your life. You get to decide what matters. How do you figure out What Really Matters? Ask yourself these questions:

1. What Really Matters (in life, love, work, or business)?

2. What did you do last week?

3. What could you do this week?

4. Of all the things you could do, what's important, what's urgent, and what is going to make you happy?

5. Of these, which do you want to get done this week?

6. If you are stuck, who can help?

What Really Matters identifies a small number of important themes or priorities in your life. This helps you evaluate your decisions and guides your choices moving forward.

Celebrate the things you finished, even if the outcomes didn't quite align with your original goal. This helps you understand where you are and helps you make better decisions about what to do next.

Reframing your to-do lists as a list of possibilities means there is no reason to feel bad if you can't do all of them this week. Most likely, some of them won't get done at all.

Your own happiness is a fully valued part of the equation. Clarifying which possibilities are important, urgent, or will make you happy lets you choose the right combination that will keep you on course. You can maintain focus on what you want to achieve. You can complete important things before they become urgent, and you can complete short-term initiatives without losing sight of long-term goals. Finally, you can ensure that you get the me-time that you need to stay happy and energized.

Write the answers on sticky notes and arrange them on the wall to visualize them. You may discover that how you are spending your time and how you want to spend your time are not in alignment with each other. You may feel that you *must* do certain things, even though you don't want to. That may be true. By ensuring that you do at least *some* things that you want to do, you take the rudder in hand and start to seize control of the situation.

These six questions do more than help you make sense of the complex situation that is your life. They also invite an attitude of kindness to yourself. You may realize you are getting more things done than you initially thought. You can remind yourself that you are doing the best you can, given the circumstances. And you can choose differently if you don't like your reality. Personal Agility helps you identify when this type of discrepancy emerges and creates space for you to remember what you want to be doing.

III. FROM LEADING YOURSELF TO LEADING OTHERS

Shweta Jaiswal is the owner of her own startup company in Gurgaon, India where she is an Agile consultant and coach. Shweta is also passionate about traveling. In 2018, Shweta quit her job of 15 years to start her firm. "I wanted to turn my passion into my profession to empower and transform people. I thought being my own boss would make my life easier. I was confronted with many different activities: product marketing, website creation, accounting, etc... I had too much to do. It was overwhelming and it was impacting my personal life. I didn't have time for my kids. Everything seemed very important, but I was not able to get closure on things. The company was not growing, and I was not getting any return on my investment. I was wondering whether quitting my job was the right decision."

Shweta decided she wanted to be more organized and able to prioritize her work. She wanted to strike a better work-life balance and bring her level of stress down. She wanted the company to be more successful. Shweta began applying Personal Agility.

"PAS brought a new discipline into my life. I used the PAS Priorities Map and Breadcrumb Trail to gain clarity. I don't miss important things. The Breadcrumb Trail helps me with reflection and retrospection so I can see what I have done and can ask myself what I could do better. It helps me not to miss important work, whether personal or professional. I update it every week and look at it every night to see that I did what I intended to do."

"On Fridays, I look at my PAS Priorities Map and feel a sense of accomplishment for what I have done (and it is really motivating). Every two months or so, I reward myself with a short vacation because I have usually accomplished so much more than I thought I could. A sense of achievement gives you happiness."

Shweta began feeling that her life was getting sorted out. She was feeling organized and structured. Her life no longer felt like a messy picture. Learning to prioritize helped her improve her work-life balance, her family situation, and her overall happiness. "The Personal Agility approach became my lifestyle. I don't have to put any extra effort into doing it. It's just part of the flow. I automatically reflect on whether something is important or not. I became a better decision-maker."

Shweta's company was successful. In one year, she established a good client base. Her company expanded beyond just training and consulting into workshops, one-to-one coaching, and cultural transformations. "The more you feel sorted, the more you can start growing into other areas. So, I can now hire people to help. People want to work with me because they know they will grow with me."

For Shweta, starting her own business had an impact on her family life, her time, and availability. As she grew her business, it was important to share her vision, ensure the people she hired were all in alignment, and that the direction was clear.

Identifying What Really Matters can involve others. At home, you have your family members and friends. At work, you have customers, stakeholders, managers, the executive board, other departments, and other people who may all have a say in What Really Matters. To move forward, you need alignment and consensus.

When two people agree on What Really Matters, then the same underlying priorities drive their decision-making; in other words, they become aligned. When you reach agreement on What Really Matters, you create alignment in your organization. PAS builds on the Six Powerful Questions with additional tools to enable others to solve problems, identify consensus, and build agreement on a course of action.

A relationship describes how individuals interact with each other. Some relationships are supportive, some neutral, and others toxic. The interactions make the difference. Simple rules of engagement enable you to define those relationships.

Emergence is the process by which individuals interact with each other to create something bigger than themselves. Individuals can form a team; teams form a league; households form a neighborhood; neighborhoods form a city, etc.

Personal Agility uses clarity of purpose, i.e., What Really Matters, and simple rules of engagement to provide direction and shape behavior.

Have you ever been in a situation in which a project's stakeholders are arguing with each other or appear to be in deep conflict? In most cases, they are 80% or 90% in agreement, but have lost sight of what they agree on. They spend their time arguing with each other about the 10% they disagree on. Each is convinced that the other has not heard them, so they repeat their positions, in an ever-louder tone of voice. And they cut each other off, saying, "I know what you're going to say..." Do you recognize this pattern?

It's ironic, but if you want people to listen to you, the best thing to do is first listen to them. *Really* listen to the other person. Let them finish not just their sentences, but also their thoughts. Ask clarifying questions. Ask if you have understood them. Ask if there is anything else. By really listening to them, you set the stage for them to listen to you. By listening to all your stakeholders, you build an understanding of the whole situation and create a trusting relationship with each stakeholder that allows you and them to move forward, both individually and collectively.

The key skill is dialogue. Ask clarifying and powerful questions, then really listen to the answers. With dialogue, you can create empathy, that feeling of "I listen to you, you listen to me, and we care about each other's answers." Empathy is an enabler for alignment, which in turn, enables decisiveness and focus.

Personal Agility provides you with "canvases"—collections of questions that help you apply the right dialogue for the situation—so you can identify and build alignment around What Really Matters in many different contexts. This, in turn, enables groups of people to take decisions that are supported by a broad consensus. Your team or organization can become decisive and can hold focus.

By applying Personal Agility to your life, you identify purpose, celebrate what you accomplish, and choose what you want to do. By using dialog and reflection, most people discover a kinder attitude emerges, first with themselves and then with other people.

Personal Agility gives you the tools to forge relationships, build trust and shape emergence so you can achieve what you want to achieve.

IV. WHAT MAKES PERSONAL AGILITY DIFFERENT FROM PERSONAL PRODUCTIVITY?

Personal Agility can trace its lineage through a combination of influences including Scrum, Lean, Kanban, coaching, Powerful Questions, The Responsibility Process by Christopher Avery, and the work of Simon Sinek (Start with Why), Daniel Pink (Drive), Patrick Lencioni (The Five Dysfunctions of a Team), and Tim Urban (Wait but Why, especially his writings on Procrastination, Emergence, and Elon Musk).

Five elements define PAS:

- **Purpose**: create clarity of purpose to align what you do with What Really Matters.

- **Celebration**: celebrate what you get done to understand where you are.

- **Choice**: choose what you do to ensure you are going someplace you want to go.

- **Cadence**: celebrate and choose at regular intervals to stay grounded, set achievable goals, and maintain focus on long-term goals.

- **Dialogue**: ask powerful questions to yourself and to others to build trust, understand challenges, and identify viable options.

Unlike many other methods that are defined as processes to follow, Personal Agility consists of powerful questions to ask yourself or others. We see five key benefits that you might not get elsewhere:

- **Clarity of Purpose**: this gives you the strength to say no.

- **Attitude**: Personal Agility encourages kindness and curiosity.

- **Dealing with Distractions**: life happens; PAS helps you recognize quickly when you are adrift.

- **Scalability**: you can use PAS with yourself, your family, your team, your project, or your organization.

- **Transformation**: if you want to be different than you are today, PAS will help you figure out who you want to be and then help you become that person or organization.

Lean and Kanban are about optimizing the flow of work; Personal Agility is about optimizing your actions to align with What Really Matters. Personal Agility goes deeper than just getting more things done to finding more happiness, fulfillment, and meaning in the things you do. Scrum is about organizing a team to produce more value in less time for customers; Personal Agility is about investing your time in things you care about.

If other frameworks are about getting things done, Personal Agility is about transformation. If you have a dream, PAS can help you make it come true. Although you could do it alone, the transformational power really emerges when you collaborate with others.

We invite you to think of PAS and its tools and questions like you would an old friend: someone who will always be there to help you if you need them. and not get upset if you haven't seen each other in a long time.

V. WHAT MAKES PERSONAL AGILITY A SCALABLE LEADERSHIP FRAMEWORK?

PAS is a leadership framework that enables anyone to see the "big picture" of their context and act accordingly. PAS is a scalable framework because it can handle situations at any level of the organization and even shape the culture of an organization. Personal Agility can be the foundation of a responsive organization.

Emergence refers to how individual parts of a system combine to make something larger than themselves, like people forming a team. Practitioners of Personal Agility harness emergence to enable their future selves to emerge by shaping the interactions with the people around them.

With the building blocks of purpose, celebration, choice, cadence, and dialogue, you have the tools to guide and shape emergence. Culture becomes actionable. The emergent properties of Personal Agility enable you to create a responsive organization:

- **Empathy and Kindness**: By being kinder to yourself it is easier to be kind to others. Empathy is a form of trust that is fostered by the tools of dialogue. Dialogue enables empathy, and empathy enables alignment.

- **Alignment**: By identifying consensus and reframing conflict as consensus on the need for a solution or a decision, you make it possible for stakeholders to align and decide.

- **Decisiveness**: Alignment enables decisions and cadence lowers the risk of wrong decisions. Decisions become less risky and less political.

- **Focus**: Cadence lowers the temptation to multitask. Thanks to alignment on purpose and decisions with strong support, an organization can focus on its priorities and hold that focus long enough to achieve its goals.

VI. HOW TO USE THIS BOOK

"Celebrate and choose your life!"

Janani Liyanage, Colombo, Sri Lanka

Life is an ocean, and you are the captain of your ship. You get to decide where you want to go. Even if you run into storms or delays, you can lead your ship to a safe harbor. This book will show you how.

Personal Agility is not just about organizing your tasks. It is about coaching yourself and others to figure out What Really Matters and lead life accordingly. It helps you to celebrate and choose your life.

In the next chapter, we will share proof that this approach really works. Each section contains case studies from people around the world: from students to CEOs, men and women in many different situations who have used PAS to transform their lives and work, measurably and obviously for the better.

In the subsequent chapters, we will present how PAS works and how you can apply it. Inside this book, you will learn how to:

- Get clear on What Really Matters in your life.

- Get good at getting things done.

- Overcome distractions and procrastination to achieve long-term goals.

- Use coaching techniques to help people create better outcomes.

- Align with stakeholders and important people in your life.

- Organize and focus on doing what matters.

- Apply servant-leadership to achieve organizational goals.

- Deal effectively with interruptions and unplanned events.

- Reward yourself and find joy each day.

In each chapter, you'll learn tools and techniques that are simple, easy to apply, and will bring you results. You'll get value as soon as you start using them! Our advice on how to use this book is simple: read a chapter, then start applying what you learned right away.

We also recommend that you join our online community and share your chapter-by-chapter experiences in our discussion group "Applying Personal Agility" at www.PersonalAgilityInstitute.org.

As you think of Personal Agility as a GPS navigator for your life or project, it connects who you are with what you do and who you are becoming. You can understand the forces in your life and where they will take you. You get to decide. These six questions can change your life.

CHAPTER 2.
THE PROMISE OF PERSONAL AGILITY

In this chapter, you will learn about the potential Personal Agility has to change your life by exploring the experiences of three individuals in three different scenarios. Each of these people have, with the assistance of personal coaches, worked through the PAS and used it to overhaul the way they organize their day-to-day lives, their businesses, their relationships, and their understanding of What Really Matters in life.

First, you will learn about Sharon Guerin, who went from struggling while working five jobs to managing her own dream business. Next, you will discover Sara A, who experienced a period of long-term unemployment, discovered PAS, and used what she learned to embark on a new and meaningful career. Finally, you will be introduced to Pete Blum, who used Personal Agility to find purpose and personal fulfillment after a career in the military.

Along the way, you will discover how each of these people represent large demographics of the modern adult population, and how their struggles, experiences, and successes mirror those of so many struggling to navigate today's increasingly complex and volatile world.

> *"Personal Agility helped me create a life I thought I'd never have."*
>
> **Sharon Guerin, Palm Harbor, Florida**
>
> *"Before I could work on my resume, I needed to work on myself."*
>
> **Sara A., Switzerland**

Even in the earliest days of developing and coaching Personal Agility, we believed that PAS had remarkable potential to help people improve their lives by increasing their effectiveness and insight. Even so, we are continually surprised by the incredible results many of our clients' experiences as they work with us.

We got our first hint of PAS's true potential several years ago, as we were getting ready for a week of face-to-face collaboration. Maria had been working with Sharon Guerin and coaching her through Personal Agility to help her get started with her own business. While planning the trip, Maria and Peter exchanged a few messages:

Maria: Peter, I'd like to introduce you to Sharon. She wants to invite us over for dinner.

Peter: Why invite us to dinner?

Maria: To say thank you.

Peter: To thank us for what?

Maria: To thank us for Personal Agility. Thanks to PAS, and our work together, she has completely turned her life around.

Over dinner, Sharon shared her story. Before, she was struggling to get by while working five jobs. Today, she is living her dream as a successful business owner. As we listened to Sharon's story, we realized that PAS had tremendous potential to help millions of people, beyond its applications in business. We decided that we needed to document more stories to uncover the potential of Personal Agility. Imagine the impact on lives if we could replicate these cases around the country and around the world!

As a result of these early case studies, we have identified at least three major societal challenges where PAS could have a move-the-needle impact on improving quality of life: people struggling to keep their head above water; people going through involuntary career-related transitions; and people returning to civilian life after military service.

In this chapter, we'll explore how three individuals—Sharon Guerin, Sara A, and Pete Blum—have applied PAS to achieve major improvements in their quality of life. We will then look at the bigger societal picture to understand the potential of applying these techniques systematically. In Part Two of this book, we will move on to cover business-related cases.

I. GOING FROM STRUGGLING TO THRIVING WITH PAS

Sharon Guerin was an aspiring private chef in St Petersburg, Florida who had dreams of starting a business but didn't know where to begin. Most of her life was spent as a single mom, and her grown kids still relied heavily on her. Despite working five jobs, she struggled to make ends meet and barely got by. She felt stuck, and unable to break the cycle that was keeping her down.

One of those jobs was driving an Uber, and this is how she met Maria. When she happened to pick Maria up from an airport in Tampa, FL, Sharon mentioned, "I would really like to become a private chef and have a TV cooking show." This off-handed comment started a conversation and led Maria and Sharon to shoot her first YouTube cooking show three days later.[2]

After launching the cooking show on YouTube, Sharon's catering business began to take off. She sought Maria's guidance in launching the business.

Initially, just financing the cost of food was a huge challenge. A missed car payment caused her car to be repossessed. Unexpected bills were a disaster. Being a single mother, she always put her family first—at the cost of her own dreams. Sharon also didn't really believe she had the ability to be successful. She was surrounded by people who were part of her roadblocks.

"I was so focused on helping my kids and making everyone else happy that I never really thought about what was important to me and where I wanted my life to go. I'd had enough of the toxic relationships and had never let go of my dreams, but I didn't have a clear path to get there. I was struggling to make any progress towards starting a successful business."

Her bank account would often get hit with fees due to insufficient funds. Usually, more money went out than came in, and she wasn't sure how to break the cycle. Sharon was open to learning and putting in the work but needed a little guidance and direction from someone who believed in her.

It was Maria alongside PAS who helped her work through those early obstacles. After two years, she had put those rocky times behind her. She could handle life's bumps like an SUV, both financially and emotionally.

When Sharon began using PAS she realized, "My roadblocks to success were not just related to business. Years of living in survival mode from challenges in my personal life are what kept me from being successful in business, in my career, and in life. Just

---

[2] *Healthy Cooking with the Culinary Queen*
https://www.youtube.com/c/TheCulinaryQueenPrivateChef

working on my business would not have been enough. I needed to make changes in my personal life."

Using Personal Agility, and by working with a coach and business partner, Sharon was able to get access to small loans that gave her the support she needed.

"Being able to visualize is essential. I identified What Really Mattered to me and created my Priorities Map. I put the three things that really mattered on sticky notes and stuck them on the dashboard of my car: health, finances, and business. See it, say it, write it. You remember it, and it becomes a habit.

"I brought on a business partner as a mentor, who shared essential know-how about running the business, from marketing and promotions to operations and invoicing—along with many other aspects of running a business. If she believed in me, I had to believe in myself, and I always kept going even when things were challenging.

"The loans enabled me to improve my cash flow, so I didn't have issues with overdraft fees. They were proof that somebody believed in me! Before, I was losing half a month's income to bank fees, so I could never get ahead. This helped me break the cycle.

"I feel more successful than I've ever felt before in my life. I feel alive. I feel loved. I feel happy. I have a stable income. My family is extremely proud of me and my growth. My kids have learned from me setting an example and are more self-sufficient than ever before. The growth of my business has given me a respected place in my community where I've catered charity events and cancer benefits for well-known organizations. I had a mindset shift when I started believing I could do it."

Sharon used to work five jobs, now she runs her dream business that brought in more than six figures in its first year of operation. This is more than twice the annual income she had ever earned. Her second year in business, landing a six-figure client was beyond her wildest dreams, yet she achieved it!

Applying Personal Agility to focus on her health led to Sharon losing more than 55 lb (25kg), and she now feels younger, healthier, and happier than she has in decades. As Sharon reflected on her achievements, she exclaimed, "I feel like my life is just beginning! What Really Matters is like the source of the tree of life. Once you know that, everything falls into place. When you have those things clearly visible, then you make your priorities, and you can dive into doing the things that help you achieve your dreams."

If the Federal Reserve board is correct, at least 40% of Americans are in a position like Sharon before she discovered Personal Agility. In 2019, 40% of Americans could not cover a $400 emergency expense and two-thirds could not handle an unexpected $1,000 expense. That's 100 to 200 million people![3]

Imagine if most people had greater control of their lives to the point where they could handle unexpected events without undue stress. PAS has already helped many clients earn more money, reject toxic relationships, and become better role models for people around them.

If this became a repeatable pattern, the impact would move the needle on national measures of income and quality of life.

If you relate to Sharon's story, you can use the tools of Personal Agility to:

- Get clear on what you truly want from your life and work
  [Chapter 3, Maximize Your Impact]
- Make your goals visible and easy to remember
  [Chapter 3, Maximize Your Impact]
- Recognize what is distracting you
  [Chapter 4, The Fastest Path]
- Find support for your journey in a coach, mentor, or friend.
  [Chapter 4, The Fastest Path]

II. USING PAS TO GO FROM UNEMPLOYEMENT TO A MEANINGFUL CAREER

Once upon a time, people would grow up, go to school, get a job, and stay employed until they retired. Today, lifetime employment is increasingly rare. People change jobs more frequently than in the past (sometimes voluntarily, sometimes not). Today, the employment market has become tougher, especially for people in the second half of their careers. Losing your job represents a cost to society and a burden on the individual. We believe Personal Agility can have a positive impact on both.

---

[3] https://www.cbsnews.com/news/nearly-40-of-americans-cant-cover-a-surprise-400-expense/

Every day when you go to work, you have things to do and people to talk to. You earn money and are "somebody." Whether you're a banker or bricklayer, a carpenter or an executive, your job gives you an identity and purpose, and fills your time. You are someone and have something to do.

The day you lose your job, everything changes. It might not be your fault, but because of that change your source of income is called into question. Once you leave work, your calendar is empty unless you fill it. No one is giving you work or telling you what to do. Filing for unemployment benefits comes with its own impacts—mental, emotional, social, and more.

You must fill your own time and get yourself organized so you can rejoin the job hunt. You'll send many applications, most of which will be rejected. A few will give you interviews. Then you must convince your new employer that you're the perfect person for the job. Every step of this process can be exhausting and disheartening... unless you have a roadmap and support.

SARA'S CASE

Sara A. previously held a senior HR Leadership position in the financial services sector while working abroad. After she left her job to settle in Switzerland, she struggled to secure a suitable position as she lacked the much-needed professional local network. "Personally, I was stuck and lost. I had not had any success applying for traditional HR jobs and the fact that I wanted to get involved in more forward-thinking company approaches made my search even more challenging.

"I wanted to find a good job where my skills and competencies would be fully utilized and appreciated, and where I could make a difference. I could do and was interested in many things, but I lacked focus. At some point I realized that I needed to define a clear target. To do this successfully, I first needed to bring order into my life. I also discovered along the way that I wanted to move away from the traditional HR scope and get more into coaching and helping people. This is something that emerged over time but is actually something I've always wanted to do.

"There is huge competition for jobs. I know what I am good at and where I could excel, but it was hard to make it clear why someone should want to hire me. Focus was a big challenge. There are so many things I could do, but I wasn't clear in my own head what I wanted.

"The competition, my lack of network, my family situation… everything made it difficult for me to focus and position myself. Without focus, you don't get past the competition. Companies often expect a lot of experience. You need to do more than convey that you are a good person for the job—you need to stand out!

"During my time as a Regional Employment Centre (RAV) Client, I was able to use the Personal Agility System to find purpose and organize myself, and thereby increase the efficiency of my job search."

Sara A. trained in PAS and started applying it right away. The program includes four weeks of follow-up coaching to help you apply Personal Agility effectively and to get value from it.

"Utilizing PAS was not just about the job search. Using PAS led me to make key decisions and turn things around in my life. I cleaned up my 'construction sites'. This changed how I put myself out there. Gaining clarity on where I wanted to be made it possible to get there. I could focus on my capabilities and values. I found my destination.

"By bringing more order and clarity into my life, I could find energy and focus. Everything comes back to What Really Matters. This is when things started falling into place with my job search as well!

"What Really Matters to me is my life, followed by time and headspace to do things I care about. I need time for my kids, my work, and to ensure that all of life's essentials get the attention they need.

"Working on myself was really important. I learned about Scrum and Agile Leadership. I finished my dissertation, though my post-graduate work did not help me find a job as much as I thought it would. I was open to coaching, but some of the coaching I received (from other sources) was unhelpful or even counterproductive. I needed to work on myself before working on my resume.

"My Agile and Scrum training was really helpful to round out my profile and get me into a company that shares the same values and practices. I could not only talk about Agility but really apply it, which was a huge advantage.

"I think the most important message of Personal Agility is to be kind to yourself. Most of my life has been about doing things for others. Focusing on what matters to me gave me a new perspective and new energy, which made me a more attractive candidate.

"Before finding a job, I gained clarity and direction. Yes, I found a good job, but more importantly, I found purpose. I realized what I wanted to be doing and could focus on that.

"Thanks to the skills I learned in the PAS training, I was able to regain my confidence and thus make a strong impression on my future employer. I found a job in a forward-thinking environment. The unemployment office could stop supporting me, and I had a job that exceeded my expectations! My Personal Agility training helped me get back into the workforce quickly!

"As Head of Human Resources, I have seen many job candidates and many performance reviews. So many people are challenged by procrastination, time management, or the need to be more productive. Having this under control will give you a huge advantage. Prioritize your actions based on What Really Matters. Apply common sense. And clean up the messes in your life. That's how you can reach your goals!"

THE POTENTIAL OF PERSONAL AGILITY - II

In Switzerland, twenty to thirty thousand people become unemployed every month. According to official statistics, if you are over 50 and don't find a job within 6 months, you probably won't ever find one. After you fall off unemployment support, you will either start your own business or live off your savings.

According to our estimates, each unemployed person in Switzerland costs an average of CHF 50,000 ($55,000 USD) to the unemployment services. Unemployment is a billion-dollar-per-month problem in a country of just eight million people.

After two years of unemployment, Sara was able to re-energize herself with Personal Agility to find new employment. PAS gave her a deep understanding of Agility, which is an in-demand skill, and the stakeholder management skills enabled her to create a relationship with her future employer and convince them that she was without a doubt the best person for the job.

What if everyone had access to these skills?

If, like Sara, you are struggling to find a new job, you can use the tools of Personal Agility to:

- Take control of your life to improve your mindset, which makes you more attractive to employers
  [Chapter 3 - Maximize Your Impact]

- Teach yourself Agility, which is an in-demand skill in many organizations, especially for people who really understand it
  [Chapter 4 - The Fastest Path]

- Learn to ask powerful questions for better results in interviews and negotiations
  [Chapter 5 - Business Coaching]

- Learn new skills and techniques, so you have up-to-date skill sets and relevant experience to talk about.
  [Chapter 3 - Maximize Your Impact]

III. TRANSITIONING FROM MILITARY SERVICE TO CIVILIAN LIFE WITH PAS

The military is more than a job. It is a way of life, a high-risk profession, and a unique culture. Members of the military constantly face potential exposure to combat situations. The military focuses on leadership, duty, trust, and teamwork—all skills which are also valuable in a civilian context.

The risks and challenges of the military can be substantial. Exposure to hazardous chemicals or violent attack, or supporting fellow soldiers in a combat situation, can take a high toll on individuals. The military has a well-thought-out approach to leadership: a combination of duty, initiative, and responsibility.

Currently 1.4 million people serve in active duty in a branch of the United States military. In addition, approximately 200,000 people enter military service every year. Most enlist straight out of high school, and about one quarter are recent college graduates. Recruits first go to boot camp, then continue with specialized training. Indoctrination builds a strong sense of identity and belonging.

After training, they go into service, where they may engage in activities around the world. Many of these engagements are highly dangerous. Permanent injury or loss of life is a real risk. Soldiers quickly take on leadership responsibilities, and it is not unusual for a young officer with four years of seniority to lead teams in battle. There is a strong culture of trust and respect. Soldiers have a sense of purpose, meaning, and camaraderie, which enables them to function, survive, and even thrive under difficult conditions.

When they leave the service, everything changes. No more jumping out of airplanes or leading people into battle. Much like the unemployed in the previous example, it is up to each former soldier to find a new purpose and meaning in their lives. Due to the extreme nature of military service, the challenge is even more daunting.

PETE BLUM'S STORY

Pete Blum is a United States military veteran, an entrepreneur, and a professional in information technology, operations, marketing, project management, and business continuity/disaster recovery. He has been a trainer, mentor, and coach to both civilians and military personnel, nationally teaching technology, social media, and entrepreneurship. His passion, mission, and focus are helping others in business and in their personal lives.

Pete spent 11 years in the U.S. military working in logistics, operations, and Information Technology (IT). After honorably completing his years of service, he transitioned into civilian life to follow his love of IT. That first year out, he had seven different jobs. He was fortunate enough to finally find a job that matched his skillset, but due to constant outsourcing, transitions to the cloud, and transformations in the IT industry, that job ended as well. His transition began again.

"The thing that sticks with you from military life even after you become a civilian are the engrained traits of sacrifice and service. As an active-duty service member or as an entrepreneur, you're always on a mission, a timeline, or an objective that must be completed before everything else. Sleeping, eating, family... who has time for that?

"My desired outcome was to either break the cycle of repeatedly transitioning as if I were still in the military by finding a great job, or starting a business that fulfilled my passion. I wanted to help others while providing stability to my family and being able to spend precious moments with them. I missed out on this while I was in the military and deployed. I wanted to never miss those moments again."

Pete used Personal Agility to take a step back and take a holistic view of his life. He realized he was spending too much time volunteering for various organizations and not enough time with his family or in paid employment. After adjusting his priorities, he got a new job with growth potential. He prioritized his health, started to work out and eat healthier, which enabled him to lose 20 pounds (9 kilos).

"In embracing PAS, I have found freedom, allowing me to spend more time with my family and focus on those treasured moments.

"I have become an entrepreneur with the ability to fulfill my passion of helping others. I can now work hard, create, shape, and guide others both personally and professionally in finding their own stability and success. Being an entrepreneur has also given me the ability to be financially free.

"Thanks to PAS, I now can share what I have learned to help transitioning military and veterans find the same personal freedom that I have achieved.

"I want to help future veterans have an easier time with transition than I did. I found myself facing a continuous cycle of work transitions, volunteering, and lack of a positive work-life balance. Most importantly, lack of focus and spreading myself too thin had a hard impact on my family, the time we spend together, and our finances as well.

"Many veterans start over in a new career or industry. From the 'life is the ocean' metaphor and finding their path, to all the other tools that PAS offers, I know from personal experience that they can have the same positive results for their lives, families, and finances as well."

THE POTENTIAL OF PERSONAL AGILITY - III

The military is an incredibly demanding occupation, but the mutual support provided during service makes everybody strong. What happens when people leave that environment?

> *"Leaving the military is like losing your identity. People either spiral up or spiral down."*
>
> **Daryl Hill, Annapolis, Maryland**

Daryl Hill, a Marine Infantry Officer, shares his perspective. "After leaving the Marines, you're still a Marine, but your environment has changed, and you are not living the same high stakes anymore. You're not going to work anymore where your coworkers will take a bullet or die for you. You enter the civilian life and are lucky to get someone to show up on time for work."

"All of sudden, your military family is gone, and it doesn't make much difference if you are leaving after four years or twenty years. Oftentimes, because of the high stakes experienced in military, your family isn't as close anymore. Your combat family is, but now they are gone. You have lost your task and your purpose and feel lost. Once you were a leader in charge of millions of dollars of equipment and hundreds of lives, and now it is hard to get a job at a hardware store. You are wondering, 'What am I supposed to do with my life?'"

Two hundred thousand people leave the US military every year, and many struggle with the transition. In fact, 6,261 US veterans committed suicide in 2019 alone.[4] Veterans are at 50% higher risk of suicide than their peers who have not served. Since 2001, more than 114,000 veterans have died by suicide. Since 2006, there has been an 86% increase in suicide rate among 18-to-34-year-old male veterans.[5]

There is no single cause for the shockingly high suicide rate among veterans, but one primary factor may be that many veterans deal with Post Traumatic Stress Disorder (PTSD). Once the parades have stopped, the PTSD remains. People are looking for something to do and something to look forward to. While many veterans get labeled as wounded warriors, it is harder to see the invisible wounds or internal suffering.

Even outside the context of the military, many people struggle to transition out of highly supportive contexts. Industry professionals, former athletes, and even retirees no longer have the identity and support that comes with being part of the organization.

What if more of them could be like Pete Blum, finding purpose through Personal Agility, while staying connected with their families, communities, and each other? The impact would not be measured in money, but in satisfied lives.

If you relate to Pete's story and you find yourself struggling mid- or post-transition, you can use the tools of Personal Agility to:

---

[4] https://blogs.va.gov/VAntage/94358/2021-national-veteran-suicide-prevention-annual-report-shows-decrease-in-veteran-suicides/
[5] https://stopsoldiersuicide.org/vet-stats

- Step back to gain clarity on your situation
  [Chapter 3 - Maximize Your Impact]

- Step into control of your life
  [Chapter 3 - Maximize Your Impact]

- Prioritize health and family, which supports your mental health
  [Chapter 3 - Maximize Your Impact]

- Embrace a mindset shift on what you can achieve
  [Chapter 3 - Maximize Your Impact]

- Make decisions that support your growth.
  [Chapter 4 - The Fastest Path & Chapter 6 - The Art of Aligning with People]

IV. SUMMARY

The patterns that have emerged through these three case studies (and the hundreds of other case studies that have informed the ongoing development of PAS) reflect major challenges posed by modern society. Just as importantly, they show how Personal Agility has helped many individuals overcome these challenges. What if we could address these challenges more systematically? What if we could enable people who are struggling with just trying to get by, unemployment, or reintegrating into civilian life to do so faster and more successfully?

Personal Agility has the potential to achieve all that, and more.

CHAPTER 3.
MAXIMIZE YOUR IMPACT

In this chapter, you will learn about how PAS can help you use your time, energy, and emotional capacity more effectively to maximize the impact you have on your career, business goals, family life, and more.

You'll begin by diving into how to successfully navigate all the smaller obstacles life throws into your path. You'll then learn how to screen out distractions and identify the most important thing you want or need to be doing at any one moment in your life.

To achieve this, you'll delve into the six questions that make up the core of Personal Agility. These relate to the key tools of the Personal Agility System, which you can use to map out where you are in your life and career, where you want to be, and how to get there.

Finally, you'll learn about the PAS Priorities Map, how it helps you organize tasks inside your home, business, or professional team, and what first steps you can take to put everything you've learned into action.

I. CASE STUDY: CLEARING OUT CHAOS

> *"The only limit to your impact is your imagination and commitment."*
>
> **Tony Robbins**

Katrina Snow was in overdrive. She was a mom. She was a project manager. She was balancing a career and her family. She had it all. And she was on the verge of burnout. "I just believed this is who I was. A type-A, go-getter, professional juggler of all things, reliable all the time to everyone, never saying no—*and* feeling that being exhausted and broken was totally normal."

Immediately following the birth of their baby, Katrina, she lost her job, and her husband suffered a back injury. During this time, she worked many small jobs—some of which paid better than others, and some not at all. She struggled to balance the demands coming from work, customers, and family. "I was living in complete chaos. I was exhausted and needed some rest.

"I was working multiple jobs and found it difficult to set boundaries. I realized I needed to stop working with toxic clients, reset my priorities, and find space to nurture myself. I wanted to stop feeling depressed, guilty, or neglectful to my friends and family. When I heard about PAS, I saw a way out."

Katrina started with the essential question of PAS—What Really Matters—and realized she wanted to get out of survival mode and get into success mode. She wanted to set boundaries and hold herself accountable in ways that were not damaging or toxic.

"PAS helped me see clearly what lay ahead. Being able to see what I could complete in a day, week, or month was life changing. It allowed me to see my life and work balance—or lack thereof—in real time. It made the chaos clear and communicable. I could identify how my actions created burnout for myself, so I could rearrange my priorities, communicate where I thought burnout would be likely, and avoid it. I was able to remove abusive, non-paying clients to make room for better clients and better pay."

Like Katrina, many of us have never-ending to-do lists, which leads to a feeling of being overwhelmed. Given that there is so much to do, prioritization becomes key. Some things matter and some things don't. Make sure the tasks that matter most are the ones you do first.

The reality is that some things simply will not get done. If you can't do everything, what things should you postpone? The least important things, the ones that will cause the least pain, regret, or cost. Strive to do the most important things first, so whatever you leave behind won't matter as much.

Personal Agility gives you a simple approach to understand What Really Matters to you. This clarity enables you to choose the most important things first. If you don't have time to do everything, you can postpone or skip the tasks with the least impact. This chapter explains how you can apply PAS to spend your time more effectively.

By getting clarity on What Really Matters and aligning her actions accordingly, Katrina was not only able to get control of the chaos in her life, but she was also able to become the person she wanted to be. You can too.

II. THE CHALLENGE OF GETTING THE RIGHT THINGS DONE

> *"Time is your most valuable currency."*
>
> **Senela Jayasuriya, Dubai, United Arab Emirates**

So many things in life seem to conspire against us, it's a wonder we get anything done at all! Between the demands of family, colleagues, friends, kids, cell phones, meetings, the latest change initiative at work and whatever else, it can be hard to focus on something long enough to get it done.

There are so many reasons why it is hard to get things done. It seems there is more to do than can fit into the small amount of time we have to accomplish our tasks. With so many competing priorities, keeping track of it all or even just deciding what to do next can be a challenge. Distractions and interruptions make it hard to stay with something to the end. We also get tired and have fears that we may or may not recognize. We are not machines.

Having impact is about the results of your work, not the quantity of your work. Personal Agility helps you get organized, identify the right things to do, and deal with whatever is holding you back.

Getting the right things done includes:

1. Setting priorities—deciding which work to do

2. Questioning—ensuring you have set the right priorities

3. Doing the actual work.

Doing work includes both the doing itself and keeping track of what needs to be done.

The purpose of asking questions is to gain clarity. Some things matter more than others, and some things don't matter at all. Are you working according to priority? If you don't know what matters, or your priorities change constantly, then you cannot consistently do the things that matter.

You may find yourself getting tired or distracted, or you may notice that you are procrastinating. When you find yourself getting off track, recognizing this enables you to do the right thing, whether that be that resting, taking action, or dealing with the cause of your procrastination. You can take action to get back on course!

Having impact is more than just achieving what you set out to achieve. Having impact results in creating alignment between what you do and the people you care about.

Meet Piyali Karmakar, a Scrum Master and Agile Coach from Bengaluru, India. Personal Agility helped her overcome her challenges with procrastination to start getting things done in a more timely manner.

"Personal Agility has taught me how to better prioritize my things. I used to have so many things at the same time. Lots of things started, everything half-done. Now I can choose what is most important for me and I can pick up things one-by-one and finish them. I can prioritize things better."

Putting things off to some future date—that may or may not come—is likely very familiar for many of us. Personal Agility helps you recover from distraction and recognize procrastination by giving you tools to visualize and prioritize your efforts. Making your progress visible helps you identify when something is not getting done and invites you to look at the real reason for delay.

III. WHAT IS THE RIGHT THING TO BE DOING NOW?

> *"Any list greater than one must be prioritized."*
>
> **Rodrigo Toledo**

When people begin using Personal Agility, there is usually something they want to change. Maybe they have a goal they want to achieve. Maybe there is something they want to change about themselves or their situation. Katrina wanted to set boundaries, feel less overwhelmed, and eliminate toxic factors in her life. Other people are happy with their situation or who they are, but want to maintain that state or deepen their understanding of themselves.

Do you know What Really Matters to you? This can be a very powerful question. Some people find it very difficult to answer. But once you know what matters, you can use this to guide your decisions about how to use your time.

There are several ways to figure out What Really Matters. You don't necessarily get the right answer on the first try. As you get a better understanding of who you are, where you are, who you want to be, and where you want to go, your "navigation stars" of What Really Matters will become clearer to you.

Here are several approaches with proven track records. You can ask yourself the following questions:

- What is your overarching goal? What do you want to accomplish?

- Who do you want to be? What is that characteristic that you want to maintain?

- What have you spent your time on? Since time is your most valuable currency, how you use your time tells you what you consider to be most important at the time you did it.

- How do you want to spend your time? Whether you see the decision driven more by choice or by obligation, your look to the future gives you another view of What Really Matters to you.

What is important to the people around you? In your personal life, this would be your family and friends. In business, these are called stakeholders. Understanding their needs and objectives can be critical to harmony and happiness at home and to your success at work.

Sometimes it just hits you. Serendipity! Suddenly you get clarity that what you thought mattered, didn't, and something else entirely does matter.

Actions speak louder than words. You only get to spend your time once. How you spend it is an important guide to What Really Matters to you.

Words matter. You can describe your future intent with different words, like how you want to, how you plan to, or how you must use your time. Which wording do you use to describe the future: want, plan, or must? Your choice of words reflects your state of mind. Your thoughts impact your words, which impact your actions, which results in the life you create.

Consider how you prioritize the things you could do. Look for patterns. What recurring themes emerge? When you recognize recurring themes, you can ask yourself whether they align with what you want to be doing.

Sometimes, you will discover that what you think matters ignores something important. You may have overlooked something essential. This recognition enables you to change the direction of your life by choosing to spend your time differently in pursuit of new, more important goals.

Sometimes you will find yourself spending time on things that don't matter. Or do they? You get to decide. Sometimes you will discover that something important is not on your radar. Sometimes the things you spend time on do matter, even though you hadn't realized it. By making your priorities and your actions visible, you can figure out what you really want to do and become more intentional in your choices.

Every time you do more of what matters and check it off your list, it's like scoring points in your favorite game. It feels rewarding. It feels empowering. And life suddenly feels more fulfilling.

IV. USING THE SIX QUESTIONS OF PERSONAL AGILITY

In Chapter 1, we introduced the Six Powerful Questions at the heart of PAS. How can you use these questions to organize your life according to What Really Matters? Let's review the questions:

1. What Really Matters?

2. What did you accomplish last week?

3. What could you do this week?

4. Of all those things, what's important, what's urgent and what's going to make you happy?

5. And of all those things, which ones do you want to get done this week?

6. Who can help?

Ask yourself these questions on a regular basis to make sense of your situation, understand your position, and choose your course moving forward. We recommend a weekly cadence.

Personal Agility offers a few simple tools to help you understand and work with the answers to these questions. The most important is the PAS Priorities Map, which you use to celebrate your accomplishments and choose what you want (or need!) to do next. We'll discuss how to represent this map—for example, with a whiteboard or cards—later in this chapter. Mapping your priorities makes it easy to choose what to do next and to come back to that goal when you get distracted.

The second tool of PAS, the Forces Map, enables you to keep track of the possible things you could do for each of the things that really matter. Third, the Breadcrumb

Trail enables you to see what you have accomplished. By seeing where you are coming from, you can decide if you like where you are going. Finally, the Alignment Compass helps you to see if you are on course and in alignment with What Really Matters when you step back and look at the bigger picture. These tools will be explained in more detail later in this chapter.

All these tools will be used regularly. For example, once a week (more or less), you go through the six questions and visualize the answers on your Priorities Map. We call this event "Celebrate and Choose," because that is what you do: "Celebrate" what you have gotten done, then "Choose" what you would like to accomplish next. What you get done may be different than what you originally intended, because life changes and you need to react. So, whatever you got done, write it down and celebrate it! Personal Agility helps you to celebrate and choose your life.

The six questions represent the start of some meaningful conversations with yourself. They can also represent the start of meaningful conversations with others. Of course, you can ask other questions as you go through your week.

Asking and answering the six questions regularly enables you to:

- Focus on doing the things that matter

- Know when you are moving in the right direction and when you aren't

- Course-correct when things don't go as planned

- Seek the help you need if you are stuck.

Over time, answering these six questions will become part of your unconscious competence. That means you won't even have to remind yourself to ask and answer them. It will be like taking in a breath of air.

This is your life. The priorities you set are your priorities.

V. CORE TOOLS OF THE PERSONAL AGILITY SYSTEM

> *"You drive the tool; the tool doesn't drive you."*
>
> **Richard Cheng, Washington D.C.**

Remember that life is like an ocean? The PAS tools are what will help you navigate across that ocean. The PAS Priorities Map, PAS Forces Map, the PAS Breadcrumb Trail, and the PAS Alignment Compass all continue that metaphor.

Use the PAS Priorities Map to set your course every week.

The PAS Forces Map enables long-term planning. It helps you stay focused and keep an eye on your end goals despite the winds and the waves pushing on your ship. By balancing the forces, you keep your ship (that is, your life) on course.

The PAS Breadcrumb Trail shows you what you have been doing up until now.

The PAS Alignment Compass is like looking at the GPS to see if you are on track toward your destination.

Let's look at each of these core tools in more detail.[6]

PAS PRIORITIES MAP

The Priorities Map is a guide to help you navigate toward what you really want in life. Use it to plan your activities and get things done on a day-to-day basis.

The Priorities Map consists of six columns:

- **What Really Matters** – a reminder of your top 3-4 priorities

- **Possibilities** – the answers to the question "What could I do?"

- **Urgent** – the items that must be completed soon or something bad might happen

---

[6] The Personal Agility System offers you additional tools, in particular the PAS Canvases to help you understand and guide relationships with the people around you. More about them in Part 2.

- **This Week** – the subset of possibilities that you'd really like or need to get done this week

- **Today** – the item you want to focus on today

- **Done** – the items you have finished since your last Celebrate and Choose (but have not celebrated yet)

See Figure 1 Excerpt from Maria's Priorities Map for an example.

The Priorities Map helps you answer the six questions of Personal Agility and choose your course of action, so you become the person you want to be. We suggest you reflect on the questions at least once per week and update your Priorities Map every time you get something done. Once you have set your priorities, your Priorities Map makes it easy to decide what to do next, or to get back to what you want to be doing if you have been interrupted.

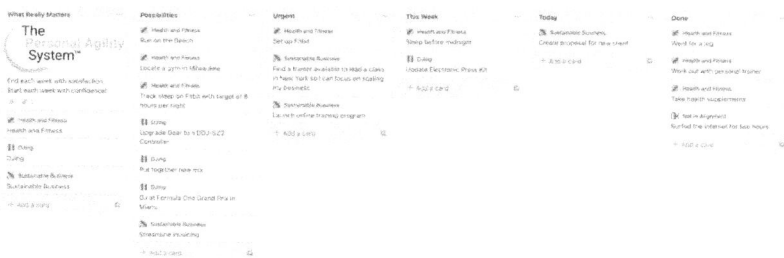

Figure 1 Excerpt from Maria's Priorities Map[7]

As you create your Priorities Map, color code the top three or four things that matter to you. As you plan out your week, the color-coding will help you visualize what you are doing, what areas you may be spending more time on, and what areas you may be neglecting. This visualization is powerful because it can be key for making decisions on what you really want to do, so you can analyze if you are spending your time in the right place.

The Priorities Map is like a good friend to whom you can always say, "What's happening?" Your friend never judges you and always supports you. If you ignore your

---

[7] High resolution graphics are available at https://personalagilityinstitute.org/book/graphics

friend for a day or two or even a couple of weeks, that's not the end of the world. You'll meet again, and your friend will always be happy to see you.

PAS FORCES MAP

If your "Possibilities" column is too long to manage, the Forces Map helps you organize of all your pending activities. Each item in your What Really Matters column corresponds to a column in the Forces Map. There may even be additional columns for specific goals or projects. You can then prioritize your tasks independently within each column, and the balance the forces as you choose which items make it into the "This Week" column of your Priorities Map. See Figure 2 for an example.

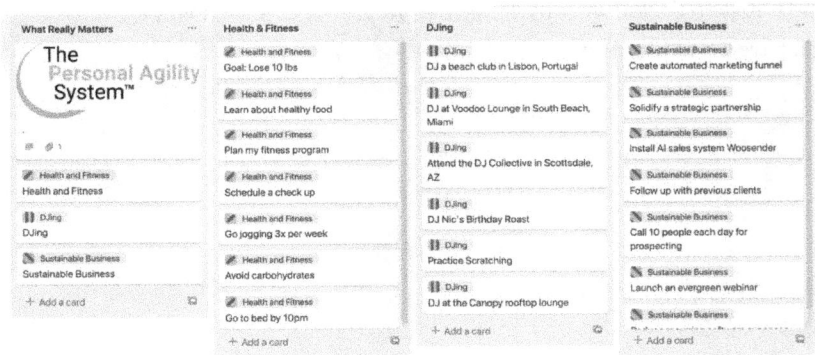

Figure 2 Excerpt from Maria's Forces Map

PAS BREADCRUMB TRAIL

The Breadcrumb Trail helps you understand where you've been, who you are, and who you are becoming. You do this by keeping track of what you accomplished when, and how these things connect to What Really Matters.

Rather than just having a single "Done" column to record completed tasks, we recommend grouping finished items by week or by month. This helps you to see what you have done over time, where you are coming from, and gives clues about where you are going. Inspired by Hansel and Gretel marking their path out of the forest, we call this path the Breadcrumb Trail.

The number of columns in the Breadcrumb Trail aligns with your cadence for doing the Celebrate and Choose event. Assuming you do it every week, you'll probably find it natural to have a column for each week of the month in the Breadcrumb Trail.

As you Celebrate and Choose, you review what you accomplished, especially the things that gave you energy or moved you forward, then transfer your cards from "Done" on the Priorities Map to the corresponding column in the Breadcrumb Trail. This is your high-five moment! Then, choose what you want to do for the next week.

Try to create cards for everything that consumes your time. You can add tasks that were unplanned directly into the "Done" column, regardless of whether you're proud of them or not (like "Went for a jog" or "Surfed the internet for two hours").

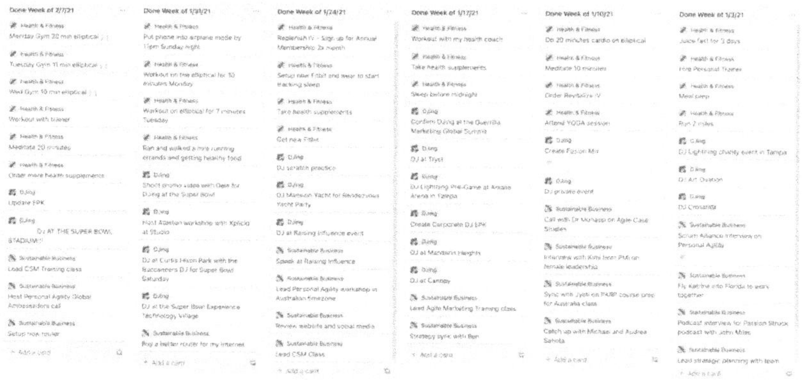

Figure 3 Excerpt from Maria's Breadcrumb Trail, Jan/Feb 2021

When you list tasks that are not aligned with What Really Matters, this can help you recognize factors that are slowing you down or pulling you off course. You may also discover something that matters that wasn't previously on your radar.

This visibility is key to helping you see and reflect on your actions and any patterns that may emerge. See Figure 3 for an example.

PAS ALIGNMENT COMPASS

While the Breadcrumb Trail helps you visualize how what you do relates to what you care about on a week-to-week basis, the PAS Alignment Compass allows you to gauge over a longer period whether what you do is aligned with What Really Matters.

By visualizing the forces in your life, you can evaluate the balance between them. Are you going where you want to go? The Alignment Compass helps you answer that question.

	2/7/21	1/31/21	1/24/21	1/17/21	1/10/21	1/3/21	Total	%
Health	6	4	4	3	4	4	25	38%
DJing	2	4	3	2	3	8	22	33%
Business	3	1	4	2	4	5	19	29%
	11	9	11	7	11	17	66	100%

Figure 4 Summary of Maria's Breadcrumb Trail

To use the Alignment Compass, simply group the cards in your "Done" column each week by the categories/color codes of What Really Matters, and then count them.

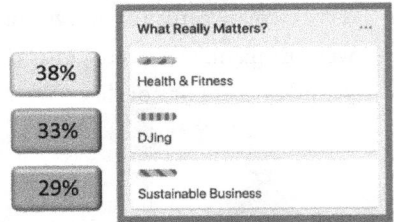

Figure 5 Totals from Maria's Breadcrumb Trail

In Figure 4, Maria has counted the cards on a week-by-week basis. Figure 5 summarizes the overall total percentages of where she spent her time. Are the forces in her life well balanced?

The Alignment Compass creates a clear visual of the attention each of your priorities is getting. To some extent it shows how much time you are spending on each priority, however this is only an approximation, because in Personal Agility, you manage tasks and priorities, not hours. See Figure 6 for an example.

We suggest you order the What Really Matters column by how much time and attention you expect to give each priority. This means that the number one item gets the most attention.

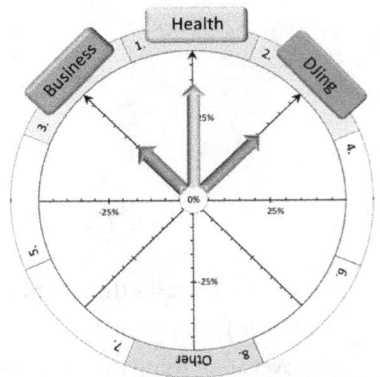

Figure 6 The Alignment Compass shows whether your actions are aligned with your priorities

By ranking each priority in this manner, the alignment will point mostly upwards if your actions are aligned with your priorities.

VI. HOW TO USE THE PAS PRIORITIES MAP

Do something for someone to serve a purpose that matters.

Human beings are very good at processing visual information. By making an abstract thing visible, you convert it into something tangible. When it is tangible, it is easier to manage. This process is called visualization. These visualization tools are called "information radiators," because, like heating radiators, they literally radiate information, making the information easy to understand and process. Some people write their to-dos on sticky notes, paste them on the wall, organize them in rows and columns, and voilà! You have an information radiator.

The PAS Priorities Map and Breadcrumb Trail are information radiators.

The first column is the What Really Matters column. The cards or sticky notes in this column do not represent individual tasks, but rather serve as "navigation stars"—permanent visual reminders of what you care about and what you want to be spending your time on. The What Really Matters column reminds you what you want to be doing.

We recommend creating a card for each of the three or four items that really matter. Create another card for your goal or purpose in using the Personal Agility System. These cards help you stay on course.

The remaining columns are used to keep track of the tasks you could do, need to do, and your plan for the week. The "Done" columns for each week in the Breadcrumb Trail show tasks that you have completed. Each card lists a task and is color coded so you can easily map each task to your 3-4 What Really Matters categories.

At the beginning of each week, you can walk through the six questions of Personal Agility and use the Priorities Map to visualize your answers:

1. What Really Matters?

This question provides guidance for deciding what to do. Ideally, what you choose to do serves some purpose that matters. The first column in the Priorities Map reminds you of what matters so you can make better decisions about what to do. You can also use this column to communicate with others about What Really Matters, especially when your priorities are changing.

The first time through, you may not be clear on what matters. If this question is hard, skip it for now and come back to it after you have answered questions two, three, and four. Then you can look for patterns that reveal where you spend your time and what you appear to value. After doing Celebrate and Choose a few times, the What Really Matters will become clearer.

When you first begin to think about What Really Matters, we recommend thinking about what change you want to make in your situation and why. Why is now the time that you want to be more focused on your true aspirations and goals?

2. What Did You Accomplish This Past Week?

At the beginning of each week, celebrate what you got done the previous week.

During the week, you will move items to the "Done" column as you finish them. At the end of the week, give yourself a high five for all the things you got done! Then move the corresponding cards to the Breadcrumb Trail. What you did can give you insights about What Really Matters from a practical perspective.

If what you did last week doesn't match with What Really Matters, adjust your planning for next week to get back on course!

3. What Could You Do?

As you collect things to do, put them in your "Possibilities" column. Then when you start the week, reflect on what you could do.

To start, just write down your to-do list. The items don't have to be in any order yet. This is the fun part where you speculate on all the things you may consider doing. (After you have gotten started, whenever you want to add a new idea, just add it to the "Possibilities" column.) At this point, we are just brainstorming.

4. What is Important, What Is Urgent, What Will Make You Happy?

First reflect on why certain things need to be finished before others, then sort the items in the "Possibilities" column according to the order in which you'd like to finish them. What do you want to get done first, what comes next, and what do you want to get done after that?

Something is important if it will help you achieve something that matters. Adding something to the "Possibilities" column does not commit you to doing it. Since your time is limited, do first the things that matter most. The goal of Personal Agility is to help you spend more time on the important stuff and less time on things that don't matter.

Something is urgent if it needs to be done soon. Typically, there is a deadline or a negative impact if these things are not done in a timely fashion. Things that are important may become urgent if you ignore them for too long. Often it is better to get things done before they become urgent! But just because something urgent crops up, that doesn't mean it is important. You still get to decide whether to do it or not.

It is okay to do things just because they make you happy. In fact, if you are not doing things for you, who will? If you often prioritize others before yourself, you are likely headed toward a burnout or some other crisis.

As most people have too much to do, choosing how to invest your time entails keeping track of what you could do, reflecting on what's important, and then deciding which things are important enough to actually do. The Priorities Map helps you to visualize everything before you decide on what to do. Use the "Possibilities" column to track what you could do.

5. What Do You Want to Accomplish This Week?

Pick the items that you really want or need to get done this week and put them in the "This Week" column. Sort them in the order you want to do them in. Put the first one in the "Today" column.

Urgent things tend to drive out important things, so to achieve your bigger goals, ensure that you spend some time on important things, even as you deal with the urgent realities of daily life. Of all the important and urgent things that you could do, what do you want to focus on? This "Choosing" is setting the course for your life.

When you have a lot to do, even deciding what to do can feel overwhelming or be a source of procrastination. Sort the cards in the order you want to do them in. Generally, the order or sequence will match their importance, though there may be some exceptions.

When you want to get something done, work on the top priority card. That will be card in the "Today" column. If you get distracted or interrupted, go back to that card. When you get it done, move it to the "Done" column, then move the next card in "This Week" to "Today" and go to work on that card.

6. Who Can Help?

This question and the answer can both help you get unstuck. If you notice that something isn't moving forward on your Priorities Map, you may want to look at why. It is okay to ask for help. For example, you might ask a friend to go to the gym with you or make a friend at the gym who also wants to train regularly.

The Celebrate and Choose event together with the Priorities Map enable you to perform triage on what you could do, so you can identify and choose to spend more time on things you care about and less time on things you don't care about. Each week brings you a step closer to achieving your goals and the person that you want to become.

VII. HOW TO USE THE PAS FORCES MAP

The Forces Map helps you when your "Possibilities" column contains so many things that you can't keep track of them all. Use the Forces Map to keep track of your "Possibilities" based on What Really Matters.

For example, if "Health and Fitness" is an element of What Really Matters, then it gets a column in the Forces Map. Let's say you have a goal to lose 10 lbs. (5 kg). Make a card for it and put it at the top of the Health and Fitness column. That's a friendly reminder what you want to achieve.

Some tasks might be things you do once, like "learn about healthy food," "plan my fitness program," or "schedule a check-up." When you are ready to do them, move them into the "This Week" column.

Other tasks might be things you will do repeatedly, like "go jogging three times per week." You can use the Forces Map to store a template for each week, with checkboxes for the three times go jogging. At your weekly Celebrate and Choose event, copy the card into the "This Week" column, and then check a box each time you go jogging.

Some things are not really tasks to do, but rather influence how you do them, like "avoid carbohydrates" or "go to bed by 10pm." You are still going to eat, and you are still going to go to bed every night, but you want to do them differently. For items like these, an information radiator can be helpful. Write them down on sticky notes and paste it someplace you will see it and appropriate moment. "Avoid carbs" might be on the refrigerator door. What is your best place for a friendly reminder that you want to go to bed by 10pm?

VIII. GETTING STARTED

Getting started with Personal Agility means going through the six questions and writing down your answers on a card (either a physical sticky-note or electronically) so you can make your answers visible on your Priorities Map.

CREATING YOUR PRIORITIES MAP

As you get ready to create your Priorities Map, the first thing you're going to do is decide where you will put it. If you want to create a physical Priorities Map, look for space on the wall in your kitchen, office, or another prominent area—somewhere where you will see it regularly. Ideally this is a space that belongs to you.

You might be thinking, "I'm not so sure I want to put something on a board on the wall because someone else might see it." You decide what's comfortable. You could do it on your computer, or print a small Priorities Map[8] so that you can keep it in a folder, take it with you and add to it while on the go. The most important idea is that you want it to be easy to access and update, so place it somewhere you look at frequently.

For example, Peter and Maria both use an online program.[9] It works for them because they both spend a lot of time on their computers, especially when traveling. If you don't have a need to carry your Priorities Map with you, then you can use a physical board that is more visible. When you see it, it should immediately remind you, "Oh yeah! This is what's important to me." These spontaneous encounters with your board are friendly reminders.

---

[8] Templates provided at www.PersonalAgilityInstitute.org/freetools
[9] People use several different tools. Trello, Miro, Mural, Excel, Google Sheets, and of course sticky notes on a physical board are all popular choices. The Personal Agility Institute offers several templates. www.personalagilityinstitute.org/dashboard/ (registration required)

WHAT REALLY MATTERS?

Think about why you are doing this. What is the goal you want to achieve, the person you want to become, or the state you want to maintain? As you identify your "Why," write it down on a card. This reflects your deeper motivation for applying Personal Agility.

If the answer to "Why" is represented by "Jamaica," then the other cards in What Really Matters correspond to navigation stars. Identify the top three to four priorities and add them to the What Really Matters column.

We recommend limiting this list of What Really Matters to three or four items. If everything matters, then nothing matters. If you have more than four items, it becomes difficult to make progress in multiple directions at once. When using Agile at work, some people will focus on limiting the amount of work in progress. We recommend limiting the number of initiatives that are in progress so that you can achieve meaningful results.

YOUR FIRST CELEBRATE AND CHOOSE

Put things you have recently gotten done directly in the "Done" column for that week. If you need help remembering, use your calendar, old to-do lists, emails, and text messages to figure out what you have accomplished. Put the cards you spent the most time on at the top of the list. As you celebrate what you've achieved and reflect on your progress, this may impact what you choose to do for the next week. Do you want to continue doing the same types of things next week or do you want to do something different?

Next, reflect on what you could do to fill the "Possibilities" column. Use question four (What is Important, What Is Urgent, What Will Make You Happy) to sort the cards by importance. Make the items at the top of the list the most important and/or urgent, that is, the ones you want to do first.

Use question five (What Do You Want to Accomplish This Week?) to select a doable set of cards to put in the "This Week" column. This is setting the course for your ship. You are balancing the forces in your life to make sure the boat is headed in the right direction.

Now look for what patterns emerge, and identify a few overriding themes that are important to you. Once you are happy with the "This Week" column, take the first card, put it in the "Today" column and start working on that item.

YOUR FIRST WEEK WITH PERSONAL AGILITY

As you go through the week, your cards move from "This Week" to "Today" to the "Done" column.

During the week, you focus your activities on the items in the "Today" and "This Week" columns. Which card is the most important to finish? The card in the "Today" column. After that, comes the card at the top of the "This Week" column.

Every day, take a quick look at your Priorities Map to see what is on the agenda for the day. What do you most want to get done today? Put it in the "Today" column.

When you finish that card (or any other card), move it to the "Done" column, and then focus your attention on the next card in the list.

If you get interrupted or distracted, well, that happens. When you're finished with whatever interrupted you, make a card for the interruption and put it straight into the "Done" column, so you know what happened. Then go back to the top card in the "Today" column.

By creating clarity about what to do next and what to come back to if you get distracted, you make it easy to choose and stay focused on the right objective, even if your busy day keeps distracting you with other things.

YOUR NEXT CELEBRATE AND CHOOSE

Each week, you'll repeat this Celebrate and Choose event. Review what you achieved, especially the things which moved you forward or made you happy. After you have reviewed the week, give yourself a high five and move all the cards in the "Done" column to the corresponding column for that week in the Breadcrumb Trail. The Breadcrumb Trail will have a column for each week so you can look back and see what was done. Now you are ready to start choosing your tasks for the next week.

FIND A CELEBRATION PARTNER

Especially at the beginning, we recommend meeting with someone once a week to act as your "Celebration Partner" to ask you the six questions and ensure that you actually Celebrate and Choose each week. They might ask you other questions to help you ensure that your goals for the week properly reflect your overall intent. This person can be an "accountability partner," a trusted friend, colleague, or even a professional coach.

WHAT IF YOU HAVE TOO MUCH TO DO?

If you do the most important and urgent things first, you can feel good about what you *did* complete, rather than stress about what is *not* complete. This is the "glass half full" approach.

Interruptions, distractions, procrastination, and just having too much to do can all make it challenging to get things done and be who you want to be. In the next chapter, we'll look at each of the challenges, identify possible causes, and suggest strategies for dealing with them.

CHAPTER 4.
THE FASTEST PATH

In this chapter, you'll look at how Personal Agility helps you recognize and recover from unforeseen challenges so you can achieve your goals as quickly and effectively as possible. You'll first learn how to stay on track with your goals, and how to bounce back from unexpected interruptions and distractions. You'll also learn about multitasking, and why it's a dangerous myth that only makes it harder for you to get your work done.

Next, we'll address procrastination—why we all struggle with it, and how to beat it. You'll then explore how to "stay in flow" and keep working toward your goals, no matter what obstacles or distractions appear in your path.

Finally, you'll learn what to do in the case of those truly unexpected, once-in-a-blue-moon storms that threaten to capsize your boat and derail your plans, and how you can weather the storm and emerge stronger than before.

> *"If you don't know where you're going, any road will get you there."*
>
> **Lewis Carroll**

I. CASE STUDY:
PERFORMING WITH PRECISION

Larry Pakieser has been an independent contractor based in Denver, Colorado since 2016. Prior to that, he worked for over 40 years in commercial service companies, focused on operations. His areas of expertise span everything from commercial services and fire system installation to IT Services.

"My problem was getting things done, and getting them done on time whether for personal, professional, or client projects. All my previous attempts were based on managing time. That's the nature of the services business: you come into the office and the first customer call ruins your plan for the day. As a service provider, you are focused on what matters to other people, not on what matters to you.

"I don't like unfinished work. Too many of my projects did not finish or did not finish on time. I wanted a system that was simple and robust in guiding me to delivering results ≥ 90% on-time. I wanted to select clients with projects that aligned with my idea of What Really Matters, and with clients who hold values compatible with mine.

"Since engaging in PAS, I have developed an emerging management system that is better than anything I have previously encountered. The big difference is I used to manage time, whereas now I manage my work. I can decide which tasks to do now, which to do later, and which not to do at all. With PAS, I am producing completed results at an unprecedented rate—and I'm having fun."

"[After starting with PAS,] I got into the 75-100% range for timely completions over the first four weeks. That's up from my 2020 First Quarter average of only 24% completion. And I had the clarity to walk away from one potential client because there was too much uncertainty and a huge values mismatch."

"What Really Matters is brilliant. It is simple and robust. I get instant clarity when I ask myself the question: If this activity doesn't add to What Really Matters for this day, week, or month—why am I doing it?"

> *"You achieve long term goals by having clarity and consistency. As a GPS Navigator for your life, Personal Agility helps you identify your goals and priorities, and helps you recognize and recover when you are getting off course or hitting strong resistance."*
>
> **Hartmuth G., Bern, Switzerland**

Interruptions and distractions are like crosswinds: they blow you off course, but you must deal with them. Doing too many things at once—otherwise known as multitasking—uses up your energy, slows you down, and lowers your output, maybe even to the point where you get nothing done at all. Procrastination is like having the gear in neutral—the engine is making a lot of noise, but you are not moving.

When you first apply Personal Agility in your life, you learn to make use of the *Priorities Map.* This ensures you are clear on What Really Matters, what's important to get done, what's urgent, what you plan to do for the week, and what is the one task you need to focus on next for the day. We also discussed how to celebrate your achievements on a weekly basis. Getting into a rhythm or flow can really accelerate you toward achieving your goals.

> *"Priorities and things that matter to you, those things are never just siloed. They don't stand alone. Your thinking switches between those things all the time. Personal Agility helped me stop thinking about other things, but look at my life, and focus on the task at hand!"*
>
> **Hartmuth G., Bern, Switzerland**

II. STAYING ON TRACK WITH YOUR GOALS

Have you ever thought about starting your own business, or considered climbing Mt. Everest? At some point your wishful dream becomes a concrete goal. What do you need to do to accomplish that goal?

Important goals often take a long time to achieve. We polled the participants of the 2018 Global Scrum Gathering in Minneapolis and asked the question, "What is a goal you always wanted to achieve?" The responses began streaming across the presentation screen, including topics from health and fitness to hobbies, career growth, or starting a business.

When we asked the audience, "How long ago did you set this goal?" 70% of people responded they had been working on their goals for a year or more, the majority of which had been working on their goals for three years or more.

Next, we asked, "What is preventing you from achieving your goals?" Only 26% said they were actively trying to achieve their goals. The other 74% put others before themselves, didn't really think about their goals, or didn't really believe they could achieve them.

Time flies! If you lose focus on your long-term goals, a year will flash by before you know it, and you won't have accomplished anything.

What do you need to do to achieve your goals? 1) Believe you can. 2) Work toward achieving them. If you get distracted, repeat step 2. If that doesn't help, you may want to re-evaluate how important this goal really is to you.

You might want to improve your health, but when you reflect on your day, you realize you didn't get your workout in. "I wanted to go to the gym," you say, making rationalizations and justifications, "but I had to run some errands and ran out of time." You may want to start your dream business but can't seem to take the first step. "I can't afford to miss a paycheck, so I spend all my time at work and my business idea never gets off the ground." These things may all be true, but that doesn't mean they aren't excuses.

Urgent things are what keep the boat from sinking. Important things are what help you reach your ultimate destination. If you never spend any time on important things, when will you do them? What happens when you use your time to do things that don't matter as much to you?

You are the captain of your boat. You set the course. If you get caught in a storm, you can't let the boat sink. Urgent things tend to push important things out of the way. Did you really have to do those errands at that moment? Do you really want to go to the gym? If it's truly important, you will find a way!

Remember to be kind to yourself. You are always doing the best that you can, given the situation at hand.

To stay on track, you first need to recognize when you are getting off track and why. Your weekly Celebrate and Choose event combined with reviewing the Breadcrumb Trail helps you do this. If you see too many things in the "Done" column that don't serve your most important goals, or if during the week you added too many things that weren't planned, these could be signs that you are drifting off course because you are not doing what serves your goals.

On the other hand, getting things done means focusing on and finishing one thing before you move on to the next thing. If things stay in the "Today" column but never reach the "Done" column, divide them into smaller, clearer steps that you can easily check off on your Priorities Map. These are easy to celebrate at the end of the week and give you a feeling of progress!

III. DEALING WITH INTERRUPTIONS AND DISTRACTIONS

When was the last time you set out to do something only to be interrupted by a phone call or instant message? Your son needs help with his homework, or your manager needs you to deal with an emergency... Interruptions are a fact of life. Every time you open Facebook or pick up your phone, you are confronted by dozens of messages and notifications that all say, "Click me!" How can you get anything done with all this noise? And if you do get distracted, how do you get back on track?

Interruptions come in many flavors. Some are important, some are urgent, and many are a waste of time.

What if the interruption is important? If you find that you need to suddenly switch tasks, if you decide that it is important and urgent enough to do right away, it's okay to do it. You get to decide what matters, and you get to change your mind when the situation changes. The choices you made at the beginning of the week set your intentions for the week, and when you get distracted, this is what you come back to. But life happens faster than you can plan. When that happens, decide what's best to do, and update your Priorities Map accordingly.

What happens if you get distracted and click on one of those tempting notifications in the browser or on your smartphone? This may be a sign that you need to take a break. It's hard to focus when you're tired, so pause, breathe, relax for a while, and when you are ready to start work again, go back to the (top) item in the "Today" column of your Priorities Map. (It can also be helpful to set your phone on airplane mode, install an adblocker, turn off notifications, or otherwise turn down the noise coming from your devices.)

What if someone comes to you with a request that is urgent, but not important enough to do right away? Does being urgent also make it important? Not necessarily. Will it sink your boat? You get to make the call as to whether it's important enough to justify doing it anyway.

Another alternative is to simply tell them you'll add it to your to-do list and put it on your Priorities Map, or even your Forces Map. Whether you put it high or low on the list depends on how important you think it is or how soon you want to work on it.

You might even just say "no." You'd like to help, but if it doesn't align with What Really Matters to you, then you are "unlikely" to get to it soon. If you do make time for something new, it will take time away from what is important to you. Whether you realize it or not, your ship is changing course. Do you want to go there?

Knowing What Really Matters enables you to explain why you said no. "Yes, I'd like to help you with ABC, but I am committed to the XYZ goal. Working on ABC would slow my progress on XYZ, and I won't be able to work on ABC and also get XYZ completed in time."

You don't have to say yes to everything. Just because someone asked you to do something doesn't mean you have to do it. If you have personal goals, it is okay to prioritize yourself and what is important to *you*. Quality of life is also important.

The Priorities Map makes it easy to recognize what you want to be doing. Whenever you get distracted, go back to the top item of "Today" in your Priorities Map. When you finish an item, move it to "Done", and go on to the next item on the list.

As you move forward, remember to be nice to yourself. The items you put in the "This Week" column don't represent a plan or a commitment, they represent the course you have set for the week. By the end of the week, you will have done some things that weren't planned but not done other things that you had intended. This is normal.

Your next Celebrate and Choose event is an opportunity to celebrate that your boat hasn't sunk and to stop and reflect on where you're heading. This gives you space for noticing whether you are really doing the things you want to be doing. If you get blown off course, use your Priorities Map to recognize that, then reset your course toward your goal.

When you find that you have done something unexpected, i.e., something that was not on your Priorities Map, it is important to write it down and put it in the "Done this week" column because this makes it visible. You can acknowledge that a) you decided that something was important, and b) you got it done. You can reflect later whether you would like to decide differently the next time that happens.

When you get to your weekly Celebrate and Choose event, celebrate *everything* you've achieved, even the things that were not in your "This Week" column at the start of the week.

IV. THE MYTH OF MULTITASKING

> *"Most of the time multitasking is an illusion. You think you are multitasking, but in reality, you're actually wasting time switching from one task to another."*
>
> **Professor Bosco Tjan**

How many projects are you working on right now? Do you believe that juggling multiple things at once is a valuable skill? Is working on multiple projects simultaneously good for your performance, or detrimental?

When you divide your time between multiple activities, this is called multitasking. Multitasking dramatically reduces the amount of time you have available to work on each individual goal. Harvard Business Review author Peter Bergman reported that multitasking leads to as much as a 40% drop in productivity.[10]

When too many things matter, nothing matters. If you are working on too many things, then you risk not completing anything.

THE IMPACT OF MULTITASKING

> *"In today's fast-paced, knowledge-based business world, it's not uncommon to see project managers juggling as many as ten IT projects simultaneously—with all types of complexities, durations, and sizes."*
>
> **Jason Charvat[11]**

How much does multitasking slow you down? If a project by itself takes one week but you have two projects to do simultaneously, what is the expense of switching back and forth between them? Working on two projects at the same time instead of one will reduce your speed by at least 50%. You will need at least twice as long to complete either project.

---

[10] Bergman, P. (2010, May 20). *How (and why) to stop multitasking.* Harvard Business Review. https://hbr.org/2010/05/how-and-why-to-stop-multitaski

[11] Charvat, J. (2003, Feb 20), *How to manage multiple IT projects,* Tech Republic

How much impact does multitasking have on your performance? There are two ways to look at this. The first way is to ask, how fast are you? How long does it take you to get one task done? The other way is to look at how much work you can get done over a certain period, say, a month or a year.

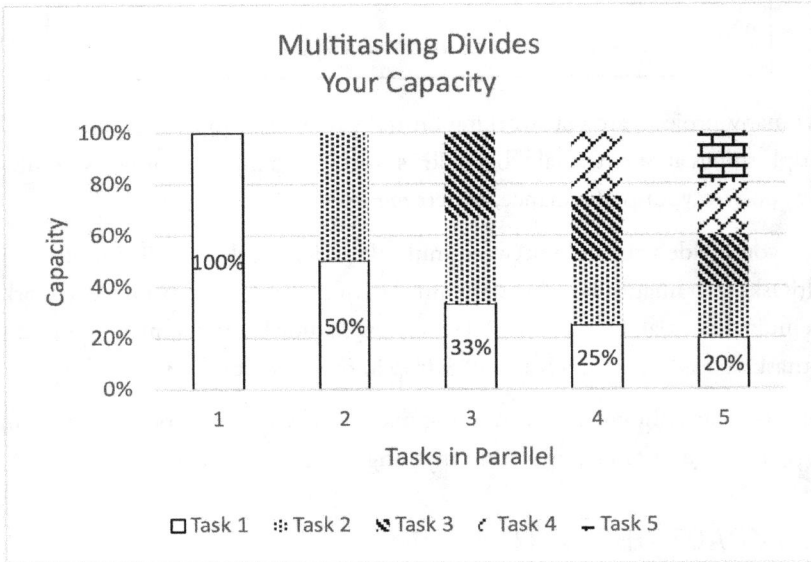

Figure 7 Multitasking Does Not Give You More Capacity

Regardless of how you look at it, multitasking is bad for your performance. The more you multitask, the more dramatically your ability to get things done declines. People may perceive that you are slow and ineffective, even though you are working very hard toward achieving your goals.

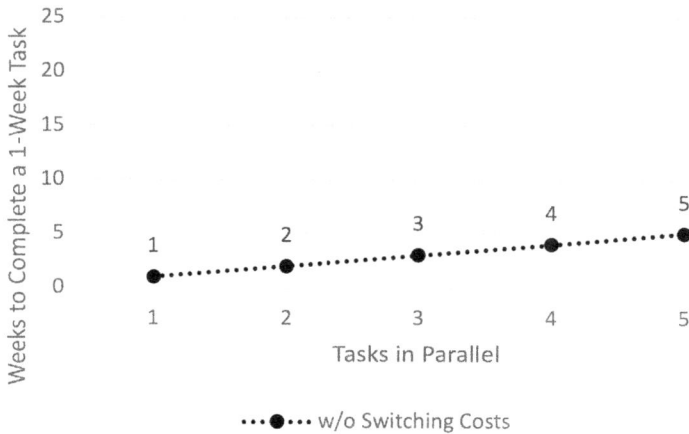

Impact of Multitasking
on Completion Time

Figure 8 Multitasking slows you down

As dramatic as these slowdown estimates are, they are quite optimistic because they do not consider the waste and cost of switching tasks. In other words, however bad you think the impacts of multitasking are on your productivity, they're probably worse still.

THE TRUE COST OF MULTITASKING

> *"Doing more than one thing at a time makes you slower and worse at both tasks."*
>
> **Jeff Sutherland**

Research by Gerald Weinberg suggests that if you are switching between two tasks, 20% of your time is lost to switching costs.[12] For each additional task you try to accomplish in parallel, you lose another 20%. By the time you have five projects going at once, you are losing around 75% of your total capacity.

---

[12] Gerald Weinberg, Weinberg, Gerald M. *Quality Software Management* (New York: Dorset House, 1991).

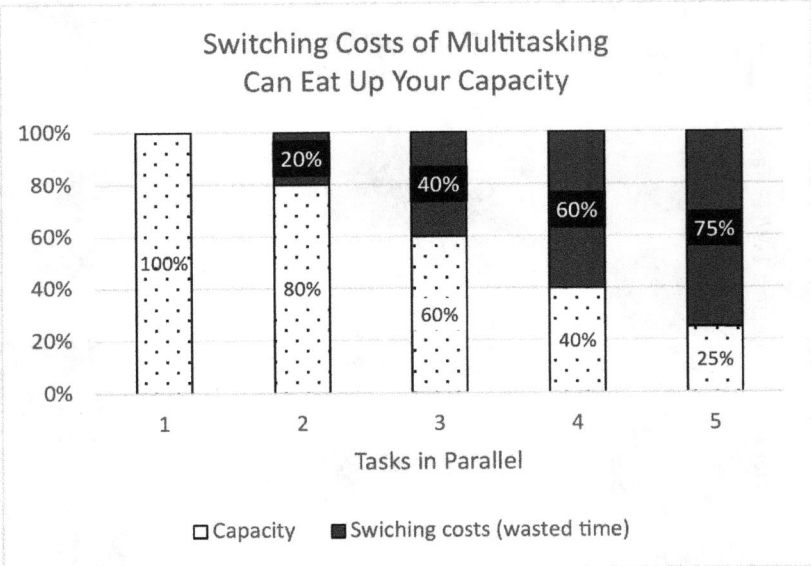

Figure 9 Multitasking reduces your capacity to do actual work

So not only have you reduced the time available to each project from 100% down to 20%, you have also wasted three quarters of that time on switching costs. In other words, you only have 5% of your time available for real work on each task. It could take you five or six months to do what you could have done in a week!

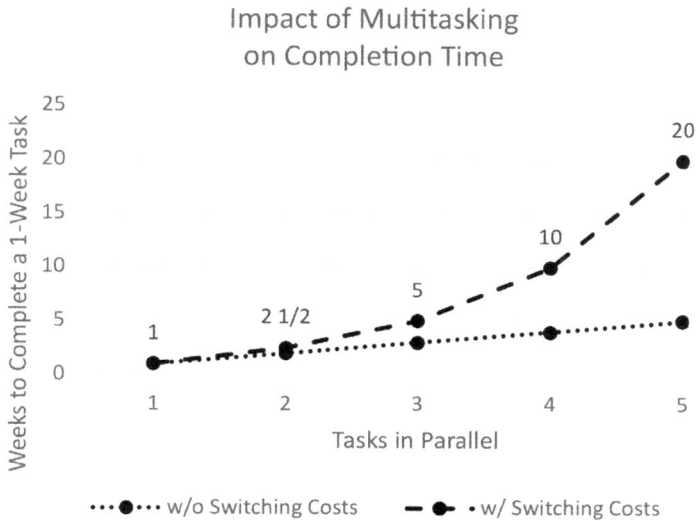

Figure 10 Switching costs make the impact of multitasking much worse

Every time you reduce the number of tasks you are multitasking by one, you double the rate at which you get things done.

> "We had 30 initiatives to improve the company and 30 people to implement them. In two years, none of them got done."
>
> **Walter Stulzer, Zurich, Switzerland**

Many articles have been written explaining why switching costs are so high. They tend to focus on the brain, and how switching from one task to another can be expensive. When you change tasks, how long does it take you to get back in the flow? Oddly enough, some kinds of task switching are very expensive while others are quite easy to do. Context switching alone doesn't seem to explain why the cost increases so dramatically with the number of tasks to perform in parallel.

Based on our experience and the reports of our users, we believe there is another explanation. Multitasking introduces a new activity: deciding what to work on next. The more tasks you must choose from, the harder it is to choose, and the harder it is to make that decision stick. We call this analysis paralysis.

The more people involved in this decision-making process, the more effort will be needed to make these decisions. The process of negotiating and renegotiating priorities involving multiple stakeholders can be time-consuming, expensive, and subject to frequent revision. This can easily account for the loss of 75% of a person's productive capacity when working on five projects at once.

THE CHALLENGE OF MULTITASKING

Walter Stulzer, Executive Director of Futureworks, explained how multitasking challenged leadership's efforts to improve the company:

"We started trying to reinvent the company about three years ago. We had many ideas for improving the company, so we started implementing them... all of them... in parallel. The problem was that we had as many initiatives as people, so we struggled to make progress on any of them. Our slow progress was compounded by a lack of clarity and focus. We started things without being clear on what we were really trying to accomplish, so we changed our minds a lot, and each change meant a delay in getting that measure completed.

"After two years of no progress, we restarted the initiative as one project that focused on a few small, well-defined goals at a time. Every three weeks or so, my management and I got together to review what we had accomplished in the previous round, and to decide what we wanted to accomplish in the next round. Each of these goals had to be doable within the three weeks. We got clear on what we were trying to achieve with each measure. We never took on more than what we thought possible in that time. We continued like this. Every three weeks, we reviewed what we had accomplished, and re-evaluated what we needed to accomplish in the next round."

"Six months later, we had accomplished everything that needed to be done to achieve our initial goals. I barely recognize the company from a year ago! Half of our initial ideas proved not to be necessary, so we didn't do them. By focusing on a small number of achievable goals in a short timeframe, and by committing to getting them done in that timeframe, we were able to achieve all our goals with half the work in one quarter of the time. And the results are already visible in our finances!"

V. ACHIEVE FOCUS THROUGH CADENCE

Walter's team used cadence to get multitasking under control. Every three weeks they met as a team to review what they had accomplished and to set goals for the next three weeks. By only setting as many goals as they thought they could achieve in that time, they forced themselves to be clear on what they wanted to achieve and to prioritize their activities.

Cadence gives you the opportunity to make fine-grained decisions about what will bring value. Focus first on the things that matter most; postpone the things don't. Only take on as much as you can expect to complete.

If you have too many things on your plate, this is also a form of multitasking. Each task you think about doing is competing for your attention. As you spread yourself thinner and thinner by jumping from one task to the next, your rate of completion slows down. The more choices you have, the harder it is to decide What Really Matters, and the harder it is to make your decision stick on what to work on. You pay the price of multitasking.

If multitasking is bad for performance, why has it become such a way of life? When we look at the number of simultaneous projects people are expected to complete at work, it seems like there is no choice but to say yes to everything that is demanded of them.

In general, when we talk to people about multitasking, the discussion quickly pushes people out of their comfort zone. Modern technology has given us the ability to multitask more than ever before. It has become expected. Focus has become old-fashioned, and multitasking has become the common way of working.

Change is easy if you want to do it. It's very difficult if you don't want to do it. Like losing weight, the first step is to believe that you can do it, the second step is to decide that you want to do it, then take action.

Without cadence, it can be hard to say no. Without a way of visualizing how much you have on your plate, it can be difficult to recognize or communicate that you have too much to do. As we'll discover in Part 2, without alignment, it is hard to make decisions about what to focus on.

Admittedly, it might not be possible to get rid of multitasking entirely, nor is it even clear that you would want to. Multitasking is like weeds in the garden. If you have too many weeds, you don't get any tomatoes, so you will have to pull the weeds from time to time. But no matter how much weeding you do, they will always come back, and you will have to go weeding again next week. The question is not how to eliminate multitasking, but how to prevent it from dominating our lives to the extent that we get no work done.

What would happen if you could reduce your multitasking just a bit? Instead of five items that really matter, reduce the number of things you are doing in parallel to just four. Experience (and the math) suggests this could halve the time you need to accomplish your goal!

HOW CAN YOU REDUCE THE IMPACT OF MULTITASKING?

Many of our practitioners have experienced periods where they fly through their "This Week" column. How do they do it? They take the first task, then finish it. Then they take the next task, finish it, then go on to the next. The decision about what to do next is easy because they already made that decision during their last Celebrate and Choose event.

Limit the number of things you could potentially work on, so it's easier to choose what to do next. You can achieve this by limiting the number of items in What Really Matters to three, maybe four items, and by limiting how many items you put in the "Possibilities" column.

Finally, focus on getting things done, as the more things you have in progress, the more multitasking you are doing. Before you start working on another card, ask yourself what you could do to get the first card done.

Our top tips for reducing the impact of multitasking:

- Introduce cadence in how you work to set natural limits to the amount of work you have in progress.

- Strive to finish things before starting new things.

- Make it easy to remember what you want to return to if you are interrupted by using your Priorities Map.

- Make it easy to identify what you want to work on next when you finish something by prioritizing what's on your Priorities Map.

- Limit the number of tasks in your "Possibilities" column (use the Forces Map for longer-term planning).

- Reserve time on your calendar to work on important items.

- Hang a *do not disturb* sign on the door.

- Turn off notifications, put your phone in airplane mode, or turn it off completely.

- Close programs on your computer that you don't need for the task at hand, especially email, messaging, and social media.

- Uninstall apps from your phone that are constantly distracting you.

- Ask someone for help to finish something you are struggling to complete.

The Priorities Map is designed to help you visualize what to work on next to stay aligned with your goals. The other tips are things that have worked for us.

VI. BEATING PROCRASTINATION

> *"If it weren't for the last minute,*
> *nothing would get done."*
>
> **Rita Mae Brown**

Have you ever had a goal for the day or something important that you wanted to do, but something kept getting in the way? You keep finding other overdue tasks to complete. You can't resist the temptations of social media, news sites, and responding to notifications. You feel bad about not working on it. People are nagging you to do it. But somehow, you don't know where to start.

Procrastination is when you know what you need to do, but you don't do it. You want to go to the gym, but you find yourself cleaning the house, replying to emails, reading comments on the latest news articles, or getting lost watching suggested videos on YouTube. You find yourself doing everything but what you set out to do. You may even be very productive... on other things, but not the important things.

In Personal Agility, you can recognize procrastination when the card doesn't move. It may be stuck in the "This Week" column, or at the top of the "Possibilities" column. You may even put it in the "Today" column, but other tasks keep jumping to the top of the queue.

Procrastination is trying to tell you something. It could be as simple as needing some rest. Often it is about fear. You could be worried about what happens if you fail, or if you succeed, or if you make the wrong choice, or even if you make any choice!

When you find yourself procrastinating, the first step is to be aware that you are stuck. Personal Agility helps you do this because the important card—the one you're procrastinating on—doesn't move. If you see these symptoms, ask yourself, "Am I procrastinating? Do I want to get this done? Why am I putting this off?"

The next step is to figure out why you are stuck. If you know what the problem is, you can do something about it. What comes next depends on the reason.

The coaching approach of asking yourself powerful questions to help you understand the problem can be helpful. Let's look at some possibilities:

How is your energy level? You might be tired from a too-long work session, or from pushing yourself too hard over a longer period. The solution: time for a coffee break. It's okay to rest and relax. You can ignore your body's needs for a while, but the longer you resist the urge to rest or sleep, the longer your body will need to recover.

What's the big deal? Sometimes, when you sit down and complete the task, you find that it wasn't nearly as difficult as you thought it would be.

What will happen if you do it? A deeper fear is often the reason for not doing something. People talk about the fear of failure. What happens if you fail in your attempt? This might explain some cases, but sometimes the fear of success can be equally paralyzing.

What will happen if you succeed? If you fail in an endeavor, you will likely stay where you are. No change in your situation. If you succeed, you might become famous, get a promotion or a pay raise, get more attention, etc. But how will your friends and colleagues react? How does success fit with your self-image? Success can change your status. Maybe it could lead to conflict with your friends or co-workers.

What will happen if you don't do it? Maybe the best choice is to simply decide not to do it. If that's the case, throw away the card! It's your life, so you get to decide.

What is the optimal outcome? Some endeavors have no good outcome. If you must share some bad news, will the experience get better or worse by postponing?

Have you been here before? What is familiar? How did you get out of the situation last time? Looking back at previous challenges and successful patterns that pulled you out of the challenge could provide great insights into your current situation. What could you change this time to get out of the rut?

And then what happens? If you are worried about the consequences of doing something, ask yourself what those consequences are. And then what? What if you don't do it? Often the fear of the consequence is worse than the actual consequence. Letting go of the fear lets you move forward.

Who can help? Maybe someone with the right expertise could help you. Maybe someone who is blocking you could become an ally.

Finally, simply visualizing your progress (or lack thereof) can help you build up your resolve to overcome procrastination.

Piyali Karmakar from Bengaluru, India shares how visualization helped her move past procrastination:

"When I went through the Personal Agility course and attended the weekly calls, I realized that fear will always be there. Fear of getting out of my comfort zone. Fear of failure. If it is important for me then I must accomplish it. Pushing past the fear gets you to where you want to be.

"As I visualize my Priorities Map and my prioritized task list, I can keep in mind the most important tasks and consider 'What is the most important work for me at this moment? What is the most important of all the things I could do?' I can review my done list, like a retrospective, and see what I had planned, what I have completed and what is in the pending list. If there is something urgent that I need to do now, then I start to do it now or I move it back to the backlog overall list. I compare my work to my bandwidth and available time of what all I can accomplish in this timebox of a week and make my board visible so I can see it."

Once you become aware of your habits and patterns and recognize this, you can get better at choosing where you spend your time, and you can choose things that get you closer to your ultimate goals.

VII. STAYING IN FLOW

As you do the Celebrate and Choose event on a weekly (or even daily) basis, look at what you got done. Look at what you chose to do for the upcoming week. Do your choices align with What Really Matters? If you find yourself distracted, multitasking, or procrastinating, here is what you can do:

- Recognize that you are drifting off course.

- Celebrate that you recognized it! Now you can do something about it.

- Ask yourself, why are you being distracted? Maybe you are just tired and need rest. Your answer will guide what to do next.

- When you are ready, look at the "Today" column to remind yourself, "This is what I want to get done today!"

- Go to work on it.

Awareness that you are drifting off course makes it easier to get back on course. Pat yourself on the back for recognizing the situation! The wind that blows your boat off course is the same wind that you can use to get your boat back on course.

Sometimes it is helpful to ask yourself questions like, what is making this hard? What am I afraid of? What is a small step that I can accomplish today? The "Who can help?" question might lead you to ask someone for help, or it might help you think about the issue from a different perspective—"What would Maria do?"

Place the next small step on the top of your "This Week" column and give yourself an extra high-five when you get it done! This process also works if you are stumped by an unexpected disruption or if an unexpected opportunity presents itself.

When you know What Really Matters, your actions align in a natural rhythm. This is a flow state. It will become second nature to you to recognize what is in alignment. It becomes easier to say no to things that are not in alignment.

VIII. WEATHERING THE STORM

Sometimes things happen that are unplanned, and we get blown off course. How do you deal with this scenario when the situation is out of your hands? You can't control what happens, but you can control how you react to it.

Even in challenging times, it is both okay and necessary to take care of yourself.

First, reacquaint yourself with What Really Matters. Deal with what you need to deal with to keep the boat afloat. Engage with the people around you to ensure everyone is aligned on What Really Matters. When you can, use the "Celebrate and Choose" event to recognize when you are getting off course, so that you can take the necessary action to get back on course. Your clarity of purpose makes you a leader, so others will be willing to support and follow you even in challenging situations.

Nayomi Handunnetti is Executive Director of the Handun Villas & Restaurants in Colombo, Sri Lanka. She is globally recognized as an author, speaker and thought leader on women's entrepreneurship. She is also a wife and mother to two daughters. Her family, her health and fitness, and her business are prominent on her list of things that matter.

"The COVID-19 pandemic caused everything in our industry to come to a grinding halt. People's buying power took a heavy blow, which caused some serious rationalization of spending from luxury to essentials. There were no international flights and therefore no international tourists. Since the entire industry was affected, we had to adapt to different market dynamics.

"We needed to weather the storm. Our staff, and our suppliers needed to hold on so we could continue after the crisis passed.

"When I was introduced to the Personal Agility Recognized Practitioner (PARP) program, it transformed my life and how I managed my time. I also realized that I wasn't alone. With everything on my plate—building the business, maintaining my health and fitness, having time for my family, and having a social life—I was really struggling to pause, take a breath, and put in the effort that was required to complete tasks in a satisfying manner.

"I realized other people were struggling with the same challenges. No one got everything right. This led me to the recognition that it is okay not to be perfect. The Priorities Map helped me to plan my tasks each day. I'm now successfully planning my day for business, family time, and fitness as well as leisure.

"As a leader during this time, I became closer to my employees. The culture, Agile thinking, and the values that the organization was built upon, truly helped us survive. In my opinion, the greatest winner for us post COVID-19 is that we have created an Agile business model which can accommodate all types of guests. We have a better understanding of our customers, and we have adapted to an efficient, low-cost operational model, along with maintaining a great team."

It's inevitable that life will hold many unexpected turns and that situations will arise that blow us off course. What we can control is the ability to recognize when this is happening and get back on track as quickly as possible. When you can identify how to deal with interruptions, distractions, and procrastination, you can be proactive in addressing these winds before they alter your course. When you reduce multitasking and stay focused, you can find your state of flow.

PART TWO:
LEADING OTHERS

The 20th century saw the rise of economies of scale. Efficient tools and processes were the key to success. Demand and competition were relatively predictable, but the 90s saw the rise of the internet. The rate of change increased dramatically, and therefore complexity and unpredictability began to dominate business challenges.

The Agile Manifesto[13], created in 2001, highlighted the importance of individuals and interactions. In clear and accessible language, it explored how empowered individuals and effective interactions were the key to mastering a complex world.

The tools and processes of 20th century management were still important, but successful outcomes depend even more on effective collaboration between people. The goal is no longer just to reduce the cost of production, but to be more responsive and reduce the cost of change.

Command and control was once considered the most effective way to hold a company together. Today we have the internet, smart phones, social media, cloud-based applications, and more. They enable transparency, fast feedback, rapid response, and self-organization.

Leaders of today have better ways to organize and lead an organization than ever before. At the same time, organizations and their leaders need to be able to respond to a complex, changing world faster than ever before.

Much less management is needed to keep things under control. People can mostly do that themselves. The new challenge is responsiveness. How can people act without having to ask a manager first? How can you ensure they see the big picture and act in the interest of the company and the customer?

New challenges require a new approach, and this section will give you tools, techniques, and understandings to lead more effectively.

---

[13] *Manifesto for Agile Software Development*, http://agilemanifesto.org

In Part One we explored the five elements of the Personal Agility System to lead yourself: Purpose, Celebration, Choice, Cadence, and Dialogue. You started using the Six Powerful Questions to align your actions with your own deeper purpose.

Part Two focuses on how to combine these elements to offer a higher-performance alternative to traditional leadership. Emergence, empathy, and alignment enable decisiveness and focus. You can have more impact and your organization can become more responsive.

This section begins with an introduction to business coaching, a simple dialogue-based approach to enable effective problem solving and activate the potential of your company's talent.

We will look at alternatives to classic command and control, share a practical approach to creating empathy and how you can use it to create alignment, then show you how you can use that approach to strengthen your customer relationships.

You will also discover how cadence and alignment enable organizational decisiveness and focus. Finally, we present a vision for Executive Agility and the skills needed to lead a modern, responsive organization.

CHAPTER 5.
BUSINESS COACHING

In this chapter, you will learn about business coaching—what it is, how it differs from traditional leadership and personal coaching, why you would want to do it, and how it can benefit you.

You will discover powerful coaching tools that have useful, everyday applications. You will then learn about the coaching approach, and how you can apply it to many aspects of your life, business, and otherwise.

Next, you'll work through several coaching questions that will form a springboard to applying coaching tools for better results in your life and work. Finally, you'll learn about how to embody the change you want to see in the world, and how to begin assisting those around you.

> *"Coaching is the modern form of management."*
>
> **Pierre Neis, Zurich, Switzerland**

I. CASE STUDY:
MY OWN AGILE TRANSFORMATION

Lyssa Adkins is best known as the author of the foundational book *Coaching Agile Teams*, which connected the Scrum Master role and Professional Coaching to give definition to the profession Agile Coach. She co-founded the Agile Coaching Institute (ACI), which specialized in developing Agile coaches to become agents of organizational change. She led the development of the ACI until it was acquired by a larger organization.

Selling the company gave her a clean slate. "The key challenge I had around that time was how to reorient myself, my business, and even my public persona so that I could attract the business I wanted to attract, and so that I could do it in a way that didn't sacrifice the sustainable pace I had very willingly and arduously crafted in my life.

"I wanted clarity in how I spent my time, and to have more kindness for myself. I often didn't count the things that were in the category of joy and play and family and community and alone time and recharging as valid or real. And I needed to.

"I had to constantly remind myself that relaxation is part of the job. Rejuvenation is part of the job. You're doing work by attending to your own foundation and the resilience that you will need in the future. This is what was going on in my head.

"That created a lot more happiness and joy in my own life, or maybe just helped me notice how much happiness and joy was already in my life.

"Of all the tools that make up the Personal Agility System, what really stands out for me is the brilliant naming of the 'Celebrate and Choose' event.

"Since I was tracking all this in my Priorities Map, I could clearly see what I had accomplished. I was like, 'Oh my gosh — I can't believe I got that much done,' even though I didn't feel like I had been pushing myself. This new way of being was both more effective and more relaxed at the same time.

"Personal Agility reminded me that I do not celebrate enough. I wasn't noticing enough what I'd accomplished or the gains I'd made. I wasn't giving myself any breaks or even trying to give myself a break. I had to rewire myself around the ritual of celebrating.

"The 'Celebrate and Choose' event helped me recognize what did happen. Good, bad, or indifferent, it represents learning and reminds me that I can choose differently next time. That was huge.

"You will have different things that matter to you, you will have a different way that you're charting your course across the ocean of your life, you will have different things that become obstacles. All of this can be revealed and worked with in a kind way."

Personal Agility is a simple coaching-based framework because, unlike other approaches, it doesn't tell you what to do or how to do it. It invites you to ask questions that help you understand yourself, your stakeholders, and your situation so you can come up with good answers and use your time wisely.

In today's complex world, nobody has all the answers. The answers to the toughest questions emerge from the interactions between specialists from multiple backgrounds. The skill of a modern leader is not to have the answers but to formulate the questions, facilitate discussion, enable collaboration, and activate the intelligence in the room. This is where great answers are found.

Coaching is a powerful approach because, in its purest form, the coach doesn't provide the answers. Rather, it allows a person to reflect on what is important. It invites you to take a step back and look at the bigger picture. The answers lie within each of us. Personal Agility helps you gain clarity.

Coaching questions strive to discover the deeper "whys" behind a problem; that is, to help you figure out What Really Matters. By asking coaching questions of other people, like your spouse, your colleagues, your friends, perhaps even your children, you can create a common understanding of What Really Matters and build alignment and trust with them.

In this chapter, we will look at how coaching is different from other forms of leadership, explore the role and tools of the coach, then show how to apply these tools in routine situations. In the following chapters, we will explore how to use these tools to create alignment in your organization and strengthen relationships with your customers.

II. HOW IS COACHING DIFFERENT FROM OTHER FORMS OF LEADERSHIP?

Leaders get different names depending on the context and what is expected of them. At the risk of oversimplifying, we can talk about several different roles:

Managers solve problems and oversee other people as they implement solutions. They ensure that people are working and producing satisfactory results. They have decision-making authority, but exactly how much depends on the context. It might be better to say, managers have influence in the organization. Managers are accountable for the results of their direct reports. A key duty of a manager is to keep things under control, that is, to prevent chaos.

Consultants are hired for their expertise. Ideally, they bring the solution or "best practices" to solve a particular problem.

A **mentor** is someone who has been there before. They have not just theoretical knowledge but also practical. An external mentor can coach, share experience, and give advice, but usually does not have decision-making authority.

A **coach** is different from all these roles. A coach is interested in helping the coachee find a good solution, not in achieving a particular solution. A coach is not assumed to have the answer but is good at asking the right question at the right moment.

Coaching is becoming an important skill in business because of the ever-increasing speed and complexity of the world businesses operate in. Traditional forms of leadership were optimal for the conditions they emerged in, but today, companies need to react faster and more effectively to changing market conditions and ever-stronger competition.

A responsive company cannot rely solely on centralized decision-making. The centralized decision-makers become bottlenecks. They simply do not have the time to properly process all the information and requests that are coming in.

A key skill of a modern executive is the ability to activate the collective intelligence of their company's talent. Everyone needs to be able to see and act on the big picture. It is less about control and more about enablement. A coaching approach gives you the tools to create alignment, empower your staff, and harness their potential.

III. POWERFUL COACHING TOOLS FOR EVERYDAY USE

> *"Coaching questions can open whole new worlds. Coaching questions help people get to the meaning underlying the facts."*
>
> **Lyssa Adkins, Author, Coaching Agile Teams**

Coaching someone is different from solving their problem. Coaching is not telling someone the solution but helping them to figure out the problem for themselves. A key tool is powerful questions. These help you explore the problem, identify desired outcomes, and evaluate possible solutions. It is more powerful to discover your own insights and find your own solutions.

Wouldn't an experienced coach have the best solution? Not necessarily.

In a personal context, who is more expert in your situation than you are? No one. So as the expert, you can come up with the best solution. Coaching helps you understand the problem, identify alternatives, think through the solution, and then take the best course of action for what you really want in your life.

The basic tools of a coach begin with asking questions and listening to the answers. Not all questions are created equal.

Closed-ended questions have a *yes* or *no* answer. Salesmen often use a variation of "Would you like too big, too small, or just right?" to guide you to a sale. You can use closed-ended questions to guide a conversation to a desired outcome.

An open-ended question enables you to explore a topic. Open-ended questions usually start with a w-word, like why, who, what, or how. If you are buying a car, you might ask the salesman, "What options do people like me typically order?"

A powerful question goes a step further. Powerful questions require thinking before responding and are usually open-ended. Your question is powerful when it makes the other person stop to think before answering.

A closed-ended question is usually an attempt to guide the conversation. An open-ended question is an invitation to a discussion. A powerful question is an invitation to think.

Coaches often use two types of powerful questions: those that gather facts and those that generate insights. Facts help you to understand the situation, and insights enable you to make good decisions.

Powerful questions can be hugely effective at building trust and alignment. They work best when you are not trying to maneuver the other person to your chosen solution. When you are coaching someone, you are not trying to provide the solution. Instead, you are trying to help the other person discover the solution.

Personal Agility helps you be proactive rather than reactive. When you ask questions, listen to the answers carefully to learn what is important to the other person. In the next section, you'll see an example of how two parties can resolve a conflict by recognizing their common goal and each other's constraints.

IV. HOW TO APPLY THE COACHING APPROACH TO DAILY LIFE

Imagine a new couple that has never had a conversation on whose family to visit over the holidays. The first Christmas comes:

Kai: What shall we do for Christmas? Let's visit my family!

Alex: Your family is out of the country. That's expensive! Let's visit my family because it's less expensive, there are more people, and it's closer to where I work. I'd much rather do that than flying out of the country just to meet your three or four closest relatives while also being cut off from the work I need to do.

Kai: But I have to see my family for Christmas. I'm always with them for the holidays.

Alex: Well, maybe we just shouldn't be together for the holidays.

What happened? Neither of them opened the conversation by looking for a solution that could meet both their needs. Neither of them were looking for the best possible outcome for both parties.

Alex is trying to create a compelling argument for *why* it is better to visit his family, but goes on the attack by belittling the value of his partner seeing her closest relatives. Kai explained that visiting her family was important to her, to which he replied with a passive-aggressive threat, implying that if he can't have it his way, they would go their separate ways.

How could a coaching approach have changed the outcome? A coaching approach includes asking clarifying questions to look at the bigger picture, from which alignment can be achieved. Questions such as:

- What is important to your family?

- What alternatives do we have?

- How have you dealt with this problem previously?

- What would *you like* to do?

These are coaching questions. The first goal is to create an understanding of each other and of the possibilities. By looking at possibilities and considering alternatives, you open the door to solutions that meet the needs of both parties. When each party jumps straight to their preferred solution, the discussion can turn into a power struggle, and the positions become hardened and difficult to change. Building understanding creates a basis to find satisfying compromises or win-win solutions.

How could this conversation have played out with more of a coaching approach? It might have been possible to avoid the conflict entirely:

Alex: What would you like to do for the holidays?

Kai: It's a family tradition that we get together between Christmas and New Year's.

Alex:	I have to finish my department's sales reports by December 31. It's difficult to get away for a long trip. I won't be able to go with you.
Kai:	I don't want to be away from you for our first Christmas, but I also want to see my family.
Alex:	Hmm. What could we do?
Kai:	What if we leave well before Christmas and you return early? I might stay for New Year's, but you could come back in time to finish your reports.

With this approach, the couple starts by exploring the problem to better understand what is important to each other. They then begin exploring possible solutions. They keep assumptions out of the discussion and avoid creating hardened positions. This opens the space for clarifying questions and for understanding. Both parties want something, and the conversation is about collectively discovering the best solution rather than jumping to conclusions. When you make assumptions and jump to wrong conclusions, you can quickly find yourself caught in a downward spiral.

What happens if the conversation escalates anyway?

Alex:	What would you like to do for the holidays?
Kai:	It's a family tradition that we get together between Christmas and New Year's.
Alex:	I have to finish my department's sales reports by December 31. It's difficult to get away for a long trip. I won't be able to go with you.
Kai:	Why does it always seem that work is more important than me?
Alex:	Someone has to pay the bills! How do you expect to afford that trip?
Kai:	(takes a deep breath) Let's take a step back. What do we really want?
Alex:	To be together for our first Christmas.
Kai:	That's what I want too. What else?
Alex:	I want to keep my job.
Kai:	Well, yeah, keeping your job is important. And I would like to see my family. What could we do?

This conversation almost went off the rails. When Kai started complaining that work was more important and he emphasized the need to earn money, things could have become emotional and gone downhill from there. Taking a step back to de-escalate the situation enables them to explore the problem and other possible solutions.

By exploring the problem anew, they discovered they have a common goal—they want to be together for Christmas—and discovered their constraints—Alex is worried about his job, and Kai wants to see her family. Now that they have a common goal, they can respect each other's limits and find a solution that meets all their needs. They are aligned on the problem.

Now they can move on from exploring the problem to exploring possible solutions. Again, by looking at possibilities, they can consider multiple alternatives until the best solution emerges.

Did you notice a pattern in the conversation? He started with a question and listened to her answer. Only then did he share what he wanted to do. You will see this pattern repeat in the chapters that follow. "Listen before you talk. Ask before you tell." If you can make this pattern second nature, you will be a master of empathy and creating alignment.

Your weekly "Celebrate and Choose" event is a great opportunity to sync up, and recognize and resolve potential conflicts with your spouse, colleague, manager, or friends. The Six Questions help you figure out what you want to be doing. Can you ask other questions? Of course! These questions represent the start of a conversation, with yourself or your celebration partner. You can use that time to look at upcoming events and discuss how to handle scheduling conflicts, needs for support, the kids' activities, etc. Waiting until the last minute can add additional urgency and pressure to an already sensitive situation. When you recognize issues early, you can often deal with them before they escalate.

> *"Learning to ask clarifying questions helped me to create safety and ease with family, friends, and colleagues. By celebrating and choosing together, my husband and I discovered we could recognize potential conflict early. If we both needed the car on Thursday, we would notice that on Monday. That gives us enough time to find alternatives. And even if we only find out on Thursday, we can still ask each other clarifying questions!"*
>
> **Sabine Stevens, Zurich, Switzerland**

V. COACHING QUESTIONS TO GET YOU STARTED

The core questions of Personal Agility help you gather facts and generate insights about your life. The role of the first question changes as you use it.

Initially, What Really Matters will help you gain insight into who you are today. Later, the answers to that question (displayed in the What Really Matters column) represent who you are or who you want to be. This gives you context for making decisions about how to invest your time. If your situation changes, then What Really Matters may change too. This gives you new insight and the ability to reorient yourself according to your new priorities.

The following lists contain some suggestions to help you get started with coaching questions.

THE SIX PERSONAL AGILITY QUESTIONS FOR NAVIGATING YOUR LIFE OR PROJECT

- What Really Matters?

- What did you get done last week?

- What could you do this week?

- Which of those are important, must get done this week, or will make you happy?

- Of all those things, which do you really want to get done this week?

- If you get stuck, who can help?

QUESTIONS TO UNDERSTAND THE PROBLEM

- What is the problem you want to solve?
- What about this is difficult?
- What are you worried about?
- What have you learned from what you've tried already?

QUESTIONS TO EXPLORE POSSIBLE SOLUTIONS

- What are some possibilities?
- What else could you do?
- What does help look like?
- What are your options?
- If you had your choice, what would you do?
- How does that relate to What Really Matters?

QUESTIONS TO LEARN FROM EXPERIENCE

- What happened? (Just the facts)
- What worked well?
- What could you do differently?
- What do you want to do more of?
- What do you want to stop or do less of?
- What is puzzling?
- What will bring you the greatest benefit?
- Which do you want to start with?

QUESTIONS FOR SETTING YOUR GOALS

- What's important about doing this?

- Who is it for?

- What is the goal of it?

- What would be the most awesome possible outcome?

- What is something you can get done this week to take one step toward your larger goal?

- What is something you can get done today which will advance you toward your larger goal?

- How do you know that you have touched all the bases?

- How will you know it is done?

VI. BEING THE CHANGE YOU WANT TO SEE

Janani Liyanage is an enterprise Agile coach who is passionate about helping people embrace the Agile mindset. She became a coach because she wanted to support people on the road to their success. Janani is married with an eight-year-old son and lives in Colombo, Sri Lanka. When she started with PAS, she was working toward her certifications as a Scrum Trainer and Enterprise Coach. She wanted to connect her passion more with her profession so she could feel that she was living her purpose every day.

"As a person, I wanted to lead the life of a coach, not just do coaching. I wanted to know which opportunities would help me realize my purpose. I was doing too many things. It looked like many things were helping me achieve my purpose, but I wasn't making any progress. I needed to do some filtering to focus on what really mattered.

"I wanted to *be* my profession. To me, living the life of a coach means I want to lead an Agile life. I want to share my inspiration with more and more people. An Agile life for me means I want to do things that are meaningful and not always have to say, 'I am too busy'. We are living in uncertain and chaotic times. I want to be able to stay calm and evaluate What Really Matters so I can do the right thing. I want to be open to new ideas and new opportunities. I want to get away from being perpetually busy.

"At first, I was not able to accept that there was a problem. I would make excuses for why I wasn't changing.

"The first thing I achieved while doing the Celebrate and Choose event was awareness and acceptance. Asking myself the powerful questions of Personal Agility enabled me to take accountability for my actions. I had to do some tough negotiations with various people in my life, like my family and my employer. It became much easier to have these crucial conversations.

"I could stop making excuses, face the challenges, and act on the things that matter to me. Now it helps me to take the steps continuously. The next step is, I want to feel more accountable.

"The visualization of the PAS Priorities Map with the color codes helps me. Before, I needed someone else to appreciate my efforts. Now, with the Celebrate and Choose event, I realize it is more important to explain things to myself than to others. I can appreciate myself for the things that I did and have accountability for the things that I didn't.

"The Personal Agility System helped me build awareness and acceptance of myself. I could stop making excuses, face the challenges, and act on the things that matter to me. Now it helps me to take the steps continuously. I feel more accountable."

Janani essentially coached herself through her challenges using the powerful questions of Personal Agility. You can help someone else gain clarity in a situation, not by giving them the solution, but by asking them powerful questions.

The questions of Personal Agility also serve as a self-assessment. Are these the only questions you need? Different situations may call for additional questions.

VII. PROBLEM SOLVING WITH BUSINESS COACHING

The big difference between Business Coaching and Personal Coaching is that in business, it is not about you; it's about the work. It's about the product or the customer. The context for What Really Matters will likely be different for challenges at work.

The challenge with complex problems is that you don't know the answer before you start. This is what you have to figure out. Sometimes even figuring out the right question can be difficult.

While the exact questions might vary, the following is a proven script for coaching someone through a challenging situation:

- What is the problem you want to solve?

- Would you like some help on this? (If the answer is no, stop!)

- What is making this difficult?

- What have you tried already?

- What are possible solutions?

- What else could you do?

- Who could help you solve this problem?

The PAS Problem Solving Canvas builds on this script to guide you through the process. See Canvas 1 on page 96 for an overview, then download it and other canvases and question catalogs from the Personal Agility Institute.[14]

You may want to get familiar with these questions by asking them first with yourself, then try them with a friend or colleague, somebody you trust, then work up to your manager, customers, or stakeholders.

---

[14] http://www.PersonalAgilityInstitute.org/dashboard (Registration required)

The
Personal Agility
System™

PAS PROBLEM SOLVING CANVAS

To help somebody solve a problem, address the topics in the numbered order.

1. Coach / Coachee	2. Create Safety	3. What is the Goal?
Who is being coached? How do you get in touch with them? Who is doing the coaching?	What is your goal or purpose in this relationship? Do you have permission? What does the coachee need to feel safe? Who will make decisions?	What are you trying to achieve? What is your mission? What would be a good outcome?
4. What is the Problem?	5. Explore Alternatives	6. What's Next?
What is making this difficult? What have you already tried? What are your concerns?	What have you already considered? What else could you do? What are 20 possible ways to achieve your goal?	What resonates? Why is this alternative better than the others? What else could you do?

CHAPTER 6.
THE ART OF ALIGNING WITH PEOPLE

In this chapter, you will learn about the most complicated topic of all: other people. You'll learn why it's vital to work effectively with others, steps you can take to make yourself a better partner in life and business, and how this will affect your teams and clients.

You'll begin by learning about trust and empathy, and why it's vital to be trustworthy both in and out of business dealings. You'll explore the concept of alignment, why it matters, how to achieve alignment, and how to maintain it in the short and long term.

You'll then double back and discover why trust is the foundation of alignment in all relationships. This will be further explored by examining the creation of trust and alignment in a sales process. Finally, you'll explore how to go from building interpersonal rapport to closing the sale.

> *"When people don't unload their opinions, and feel like they've been listened to, they won't really get on board."*
>
> **Patrick Lencioni**

I. CASE STUDY:
FINDING WORK/LIFE BALANCE

Jörg Ewald had been working hard. He'd taken over a struggling small business just outside of Lucerne, Switzerland with the goal of turning it around. Eighteen months later, the company was still struggling, and finances were getting tighter. This meant reductions in staff, leaving Jörg to pick up the slack himself. There was too much to do, he was working 80+ hour weeks, and he found it difficult to prioritize.

Jörg asked Peter for help because he felt he wasn't making progress toward turning the company around. He agreed to start using Personal Agility to help him focus and achieve his goals. They got together every two weeks to "Celebrate and Choose."

The first time they worked through the "Celebrate and Choose" event, Jörg identified seven recurring themes related to running his business. These included customer support, new product development, searching for investors, partner management, sales and marketing, and a few other things. The list seemed endless, and everything was important.

Peter: Where is saving the company on your Priorities Map?

Jörg: It's all about saving the company.

Peter: Why don't you make a card that says, "Save the company"?

He created the card and made it the top priority item in his What Really Matters column.

Two weeks later, Peter and Jörg met again for another "Celebrate and Choose" session. The focus was still on saving the company, but somehow this wasn't satisfying. There was still too much to do, and progress on all fronts was slow. Still, he celebrated, he chose, and he had an idea of what he wanted to do when he left the office.

On the way home, Jörg had an epiphany! "Yes, I want to save the company, but what I really want is to have a decent life." He hurried home and shared this realization with his significant other. "Okay, so what does this mean?" she asked. Jörg thought for a moment. "Well, how about we go see a movie tonight?" She was delighted. "You haven't suggested anything like that since you took over the company!" And they went out for a movie.

Did they live happily ever after? By rethinking his priorities, Jörg let go of some key assumptions, and was able to make important changes in his life. This gave the company a second chance. He found a solution for the company and was able to allow himself more quality time, which improved his life.

Captains do not sail their ships alone.

When you are clear on What Really Matters, you can set priorities, make important decisions, and communicate them effectively to the people around you. They in turn can know what is important to you and evaluate what it means for them. They can align themselves with you and these new priorities if they choose.

Creating alignment with the people around you is a powerful way to get meaningful things done. You can use this approach in a personal, family setting, or professional context. At work, these people might be your colleagues, managers, customers, or stakeholders; at home they include your spouse, children, in-laws, other relatives, or friends. Regardless, when you are aligned, you are all pulling in the same direction without significant resistance.

We are going to use the term "stakeholders" to refer to the people around you, whether in life or work.

We will show you how to build alignment effectively, first with yourself, then with others, so that the important stakeholders in your life act as tailwinds rather than headwinds. This alignment helps you go faster.

These principles are simple and scalable, and over the next few chapters we will show you how to apply them in contexts ranging from your personal life to massive endeavors involving hundreds of thousands of people.

II. WHAT IS ALIGNMENT AND WHY DOES IT MATTER?

Imagine what it would be like if you truly felt understood and supported by all the important people in your life.

If someone asked you, "What Really Matters?" how would you respond? Does the answer roll off your tongue because you have thought about it and therefore you know where you are going and why? Or are you taken aback, grasping for words, uncertain about the right answer?

In life, each one of us gets to answer this question for ourselves. When you are clear on what matters and are aligned with yourself, you know who you are and have confidence in where you are going. You can also more easily identify whether the people around you are in alignment with what is important to you.

In business, there are more people involved in identifying which initiatives really matter. Creating alignment is about creating that feeling of being understood and supported among your stakeholders. The process of creating alignment is the process of creating trust and building agreement on What Really Matters.

When two people agree on What Really Matters, they know what is important and where they are going together. We can say they are aligned. Whenever they make decisions, they will be pulling in the same direction because they are on the same page.

If two people have different values or priorities, they may think different things matter. These differences can create conflict.

Let's take a scenario: Parents, kids, and homework. How much do you think parents should help their kids with their homework?

Dad: Kids learn by doing their homework. They won't learn if you do it for them. It's important that the kids take responsibility for doing their homework. If they don't do it, the teacher will give them bad grades, which will teach them to do better in the future.

Mom: Kids learn by example, so I try to be a role model. It's important that they do their homework and get good grades, so I sit down with them and help them with their homework because they are much more likely to do it if I do it with them.

Dad: I wish Mom would stop doing their homework for them. They're never going to learn to take responsibility that way.

Mom: I wish Dad would also take some time with the kids to help them with their homework. They're never going to learn if we don't.

If the kids have homework three times a week, how often are Mom and Dad going to have this disagreement? If they keep having the same discussion, what is going to happen to the level of conflict and frustration in their relationship?

Because of these repetitive and frustrating conversations, they may not realize how much they are aligned on the importance of the kids' learning as they do their homework. Their lack of awareness on their alignment can cause a lot of unnecessary conflict.

A conversation about the value of homework can help them figure out what they agree on. In this case, they both agree that the kids' learning is important. Agreeing on the most important things makes it easier to compromise on smaller things. Achieving alignment on What Really Matters can reduce recurring conflict.

When you are not being heard, not being taken seriously, or not being supported, how do you feel? How does that change your actions? People may act defensively, start blaming others, or disengage from the situation. Building alignment—that is, building agreement on What Really Matters—is a process of listening to each other.

We call this "Alignment Trust": I listen to you, you listen to me, and we care about each other's answers.

When alignment trust is missing, people struggle to be heard. A common symptom is cutting each other off in conversation. "I know what you're going to say! Now listen to me." When people don't feel heard, they shout louder and interrupt each other more often.

When people are aligned, they flow in the same direction. They share common priorities. When confronted with a challenge, they are much more likely to make the right decision because they are pulling towards the same goal. Alignment does not eliminate the need for coordination, but it does enable distributed and delegated decision-making.

Compare this with an organization that gives instructions based on what to do, rather than why to do it. When confronted with an unexpected situation, if people don't know what matters, they are unable to decide correctly. Either they guess, which is unlikely to produce a good result but will lead to different people doing different things, or they ask for instructions, which both slows down the decision-making process and lowers the quality of the decision.

Imagine what your life will be like once you have achieved alignment with those around you! For Ilja Thieme of Bern, Switzerland, it meant, "I'm also way better in sync with my partner—she's doing Personal Agility as well. We're coaching each other and we're very much aligned in our private lives, what matters in our life and relationships. This is the biggest impact in my private life."

III. HOW TO BE TRUSTWORTHY

Why should someone trust you? The basic skill for building trust is delivering on your commitments. In other words, doing what you say you will do. Personal Agility gives you the tools to focus on and deliver your important commitments. You learned how in Chapter Two.

While fulfilling your promises is the foundation of building trust with other people, whether at work or in your private life, the next level is alignment. As you move forward and make decisions about what to do and how to do it, the "why" drives your decision-making.

A common misconception, especially in business, is that alignment is about understanding what to do. This might work in a predictable world, but if you are confronted with something unexpected you will need to make a decision. Without understanding the deeper reasons—that is, without alignment—it can be difficult to make a good decision.

The tools to create alignment include empathy, understanding, and agreement on what is important—to understand why you do things. In Personal Agility, we call this underlying reason "What Really Matters." How can you figure out What Really Matters to someone else? This is where we borrow from the tools of the life coach, applying techniques like Powerful Questions, so you can build a common understanding of What Really Matters with those around you.

IV. HOW DO YOU ACHIEVE AND MAINTAIN ALIGNMENT?

Personal Agility can help you create alignment at home and at work, whether in personal relationships or in creating alignment in your organization.

One problem many companies are facing is that hierarchical decision-making is too slow, and the world changes by the time a decision is made. This leads to situations where people can't do anything without talking to a manager.

In a relationship, if you don't have explicit alignment, you may be surprised to discover what you don't agree on. People have different assumptions, different values, and a different understanding of the situation so they could easily make decisions that pull in different directions. The result is conflict and misunderstanding.

Let's look at three cases:

A company leader who wants his staff to be aligned with him

How does the leader of a department ensure people understand what they need to achieve? From a company perspective, the purpose of alignment is to enable effective decision-making. When everyone understands why they're doing what they're doing, they can make decisions that serve the larger purpose of the organization.

A staff member who wants to be aligned with a higher purpose

How does your part fit into the whole? How can you be sure you're doing the right thing? How can you be certain that your managers and stakeholders will support your actions and decisions? If you can understand and execute on What Really Matters, then your stakeholders can trust you to do the right thing and you don't have to ask for permission at every turn.

A husband and wife who want to have less conflict and feel like a team

How do they ensure they are on the same page? This could range from how they want to raise their kids to who is using the car on Thursday. The process of creating alignment starts with listening to each other and showing respect and interest for the other person. Doing this on a regular basis pulls partners closer together.

The basis of alignment is shared understanding. The process of creating shared understanding builds trust. Thus, the process of creating alignment is the process of creating trust. Trust can invite a level of connectedness, vulnerability, and authenticity—the willingness to be seen as human, and to know it's okay to ask for help.

Personal Agility helps you create alignment with the people around you in several ways:

- **Weekly Celebrate and Choose** - Looking at the Priorities Map, doing the weekly planning together, and looking at the calendar together can help you identify what you need from each other or flag any potential conflicts.

- **Daily Celebrate and Choose** - As you review your Priorities Map, you can invite another trusted person to join you who has an interest in your schedule or plans. At home, this could be your husband or wife; at work, this could be a business partner, your manager, or a colleague. What did you do yesterday? What is the plan for today? If you are feeling stuck, this is an opportunity to ask for help. Tip: A great way to do this is to combine this with a walk outside in the fresh air!

- **The Stakeholder Canvas**[15] - A structured interview to help you understand What Really Matters to another person and help them to understand they can trust you. This provides an organized way of listening to someone you care about. Ask them the questions one by one. After each question, read back to them what they said, and ask, "Did I understand you correctly; is there anything else?" People love this because they feel understood.

---

[15] See page 132

- **Shared purpose** - Creating shared goals and a shared vision helps to create agreement on common objectives for working toward achieving something of value.

In the next chapter, we will talk about simple rules that can guide behavior and lead to more constructive conversations.

Imagine you are working with someone, and you have high confidence that they understand you, they care about you, and that they will do what they say they are going to do. They won't forget you or let you down. How would you like to work with this person? How would you like to be this person? Personal Agility gives you the tools to build understanding with someone, keep track of what you intend to do, and be reliable when it comes to your commitments. You can be that trustworthy person.

V. TRUST AND EMPATHY
AS THE FOUNDATION OF ALIGNMENT

> *"Trust is the glue of life. It's the most essential ingredient in effective communication. It's the foundational principle that holds all relationships together."*
>
> **Stephen Covey**

Trust, Empathy, and Alignment are the building blocks of a good relationship. When you don't trust someone, you are more likely to assume the worst about their intentions. This can lead to misunderstandings, incorrect conclusions, rash decisions, escalation, and conflict.

In his book *The Five Dysfunctions of a Team*, Patrick Lencioni introduced the notion that a lack of trust is the root cause of much dysfunction in a company, especially when found in the leadership team.

Trust can mean a lot of different things. "Can I trust this person?" is a relevant question in life and business. Let's look at a couple of different ways we might understand trust:

- **Blind Trust** – Take it on faith with no ability to verify. "Don't worry, be happy." This is the scariest form of trust, especially for your manager, who is accountable for the work you do.

- **Commitment Trust** – Do you do what you say you are going to do? This is perhaps the most fundamental form of trust.

- **Confidence Trust** – Will the other person betray your confidence? Can you admit weakness or secrets, and will they stay secret? Do they say the same thing to you as they say to your manager?

- **Alliance Trust** – When the going gets tough, you'll stay loyal to me "in battle."

- **Fear-less Trust/Psychological Safety** – Trust without fear. You can admit weakness without worrying that the knowledge will be used against you. Google coined the term "psychological safety" for this aspect of trust.

To this list, we add **Alignment Trust**: I listen to you, you listen to me, and we care about each other's answers. The secret to creating alignment is truly listening to each other. Once you have really listened to them, they will be ready to listen to you.

Establishing empathy is an essential step on the road to creating alignment. Empathy is defined as "the action of understanding, being aware of, being sensitive to, and vicariously experiencing the feelings, thoughts, and experience of another..."[16] Engaging in dialogue, that is asking powerful questions and really listening to the answers, can lead to increased understanding and empathy.

Lencioni's notion of trust is essentially psychological safety. Since the latter term is now widely used, we suggest using it. Along with psychological safety, you will often hear the term "trust culture" to refer to the same thing, and "blame culture" which is the opposite. You can recognize a blame culture by the finger-pointing when things go wrong.

In business, the classical approach to getting things done is called "command and control." Managers or engineers figure out what to do, then tell workers what to do and how to do it. Later, they check that the work has been done correctly. So-called

---

[16] https://www.merriam-webster.com/dictionary/empathy

Agile methods replace command and control with trust, transparency, and fast feedback. Conversations shift from what needs to be done to "What outcomes are we trying to achieve and why?"

How can a trust-based approach be more effective than a control-based approach? When something goes wrong, a blame culture first identifies the guilty party: Who gets to suffer the consequences of the mistake? This makes people defensive and unwilling to talk about real issues. In a trust culture, people go directly to identifying the issue, the cause of the issue and how to resolve it, without going through the exercise of finding a "guilty party."

When two people agree on What Really Matters or can agree to accommodate What Really Matters to the other person, then their decisions will reflect the same objectives and priorities.

VI. CREATING TRUST AND ALIGNMENT IN A SALES PROCESS

When you start working with a potential customer, they are probably thinking, "Can I trust this person?" Your first job is to establish a rapport with them, understand them, and ensure that they know that you are listening to them.

When you want to build trust with a new customer, stakeholder, manager or future employer, here is a simple two step approach.

1. Create Alignment Trust and show empathy by asking good questions and listening to the answers.

2. Demonstrate Commitment Trust by identifying something you can do for that person quickly, committing to it, then delivering on your commitment as soon as possible.

Identifying this "low-hanging fruit" and then delivering on your commitment sends a clear message that you understand them, you care about them, and you do what you say you are going to do. You make it clear: You are trustworthy.

VII. FROM BUILDING RAPPORT
TO CLOSING THE SALE

Questions are powerful tools to guide conversations. As with any task, it is essential to use the right tool for the job. Communication is not just about what you say, it is about listening. When you are trying to build rapport, you do not want to be debating with your customer. Your true objective is to understand what the real need is.

Ask a question, then listen to ensure understanding.

Powerful, open-ended questions are useful to start the conversation and keep it moving forward. "What are you trying to accomplish?" "What is the most important goal?" "What would be an awesome outcome?" These questions help the customer figure out what they want to achieve.

Closed-ended questions guide the conversation through a process. Two of the most important closed-ended questions are:

- Have I understood you correctly?

- Is there anything else?

These both confirm your understanding and give you the opportunity to correct any misunderstandings and fill in any blind spots. They also send the message that you have really understood them and that you have heard the whole story.

Ideally, each segment of an interview ends with, "Have I understood you correctly?" – "Yes." Then you can move on to the next section. That series of small *yes* responses during the interview is also more likely to lead to a much bigger yes—the sale—at the end of the process.

As your conversation approaches a decision, a special form of closed-ended question increases the likelihood of a positive outcome. "Do you want to buy it?" This simple, closed-ended question only has two answers: yes or no. The odds are 50/50 at best. "What are the options?" A, B or C. "Which would you prefer?" Now your chances are much better, because all the options entail moving forward.

You can use this interview to understand the motivations, goals, concerns, fears, frustrations, and objectives of your future customer. Building this deep understanding is also a trust-building process, which enables you to offer better solutions.

In the next chapter, we will take a closer look at alignment and how it applies to leadership. We also will present the PAS Stakeholder Canvas, a simple guide to build alignment with your managers, customers, board members and other stakeholders.

CHAPTER 7.
THE PATH TO LEADERSHIP

In this chapter, you will take your first steps along the long road to effective, holistic leadership. A responsive organization needs to be both decisive and able to hold focus long enough to achieve its goals.

First, you'll discover the conditions needed to create this alignment. Then you will explore how Clarity of Purpose and guiding behavior through emergence enables you to create both autonomy and alignment.

Finally, you'll explore how to enable autonomy and alignment amongst teams, as well as how to create alignment with your stakeholders.

> *"The most empowering condition of all is when the entire organization is aligned with its mission, and people's passions and purposes are in sync with each other."*
>
> **Bill George**

I. CASE STUDY:
ALIGNING THE BOARD OF DIRECTORS

Michael Mrochen is the co-founder and Chairman of the Board of Vivior AG, a Swiss digital health start-up. "We were running out of money as our industry partners could not proceed with promoting our product through their channels. We needed to get the company unstuck and create the willingness to try something new. If we kept on doing what we were doing, we would fail.

"We had a roadmap to enter our markets with strategic partners. The roadmap didn't work anymore because, thanks to COVID, everything was canceled. The organization was not equipped to respond to the situation. We had three directions in which we could focus. There were huge opportunities, all had challenges, and we need to focus on one of them."

The question was, which one? "We engaged an outside coach to interview each stakeholder individually then lead us through a workshop together with the goal of deciding what to do next. The coach used the PAS Stakeholder Canvas to guide the conversations and understand each stakeholder's point of view.

"The workshop emphasized storytelling and listening. We made small working agreements, such as listening before we spoke, asking before we told, listening for understanding, and asking clarifying questions. Making small agreements in the morning enabled us to have conversations about real issues later in the day with minimal conflict."

During this time, they had working agreements in place, like "listen before you talk," "ask clarifying questions rather than debating," and "let people finish their sentences."

"We had identified a champion for each market segment, and they spent the afternoon presenting the alternatives we could focus on. Each champion made their best case, and we strove to understand their reasoning and the strengths and weaknesses of each one.

"At the end of the day, everybody voted, which resulted in a clear recommendation. Even one of the other champions voted for the winning approach. The next day, the board ratified this recommendation.

"The process of interviewing everyone with the Stakeholder Canvas created by an outsider gave us a condensed, holistic, and honest view of the situation. The process created transparency and alignment among the Board members and Chief Officers. We agreed on What Really Matters moving forward. As it became clear what we needed to do, we could all agree both on what and why, so we could move forward without resistance or hesitation."

II. ACHIEVING DECISIVENESS AND HOLDING FOCUS

What made this decision for the Vivior board possible was alignment and empathy. Really listening to each other, not to score points, but to build understanding of the problem and the alternatives. They had all the decision-makers in the room. They avoided discussions that would cause fights. After hearing the facts, they made a decision that all relevant stakeholders supported. Because everyone was present and on board, they could move forward.

Remember when Walter Stulzer was able to turn his company back to profitability in Chapter 4? Every three weeks, the leadership team got together to review their progress and set goals for the next iteration. Cadence provides regular opportunities to ensure that everyone is still aligned on the major goals and review progress towards achieving them.

Cadence enables you to hold strategic focus over long periods of time and ensure short-term focus on the most valuable activities. When major goals are achieved (or abandoned), this is a moment to step back, re-evaluate What Really Matters and set the next strategic goals.

III. ALTERNATIVES TO COMMAND AND CONTROL

> *"If you want to build a ship, don't drum up the men to gather wood, divide the work, and give orders. Instead, teach them to yearn for the vast and endless sea."*
>
> **Antoine de Saint-Exupéry**

"Stand-up! Left face! Forward march!" These, simple clear instructions are often associated with "military style" leadership. This method is often called "Command and Control." It works very well for getting the troops from here to there. However, the instructions cannot be too complicated, and as soon as any decision-making is required along the way, this method of leadership shows its limitations.

If a manager delegates a task to a staff member, they often have to validate that the task was performed correctly. If the staff member encounters something unexpected, they may have to ask for an explanation, additional instructions, or help with a decision. And when they are done, the manager may need to confirm that the work was done correctly.

Delegation is a boomerang. It has someone else do the work, but it can generate additional work for managers to confirm the work was completed properly. Managers can become bottlenecks when everyone needs their time, and they can become a single point of failure for the organization because if they are not available, nothing moves.

Delegation can turn management time into a scarce resource. The higher you are in the organization, the less time you have for the issues of your direct reports (and their direct reports, etc.) When many initiatives that depend on you are forced to wait until you have time for them, this can impede decision-making and make it difficult for the organization to respond to new situations.

An extreme form of command and control is micromanagement. The manager may believe their staff are not capable of seeing the big picture. Conversely, the staff may not engage fully, thinking, "My boss will probably want something different anyway, so why not wait to be told what is really needed?" Eventually, micromanagement can become a self-fulfilling prophecy, even a belief system. We have met so many managers who find it hard to believe that employees can take responsibility, not realizing that micromanaging discourages their staff from doing so.

Sometimes it is necessary to stand down, get out of the way, and let people work. Sometimes they even need to fail to learn from the experience.

If micromanagement represents an excess of command and control, what are the alternatives? Some approaches do not require active control at all:

- **Invitation, Example and Celebration:** Derek Sivers talks about "How to Start a Movement" in his well-known TED Talk[17] where he narrates a video of a guy dancing alone who attracts hundreds of others to join in. If you want people to dance, start dancing! Invite others to join you. Lead by example and celebrate your "first followers" who join you in the dance.

  You can apply this approach when you start using PAS. Just put your Priorities Map on the wall in your office. Show your friends, colleagues, and staff how you prioritize things and how it helps you. Give them encouragement as they get started. Your enthusiasm will be contagious!

- **The X-Prize approach**: Hang out a carrot, let people respond. X-Prize is a non-profit organization that designs and hosts public competitions intended to encourage technological development to benefit humanity.[18] The Ten-million-dollar Ansari X Prize inspired Scaled Composites and 25 other projects to try to create a reusable spacecraft that can carry passengers into space and repeat the feat in a few days.[19]

---

[17] https://www.ted.com/talks/derek_sivers_how_to_start_a_movement
[18] https://en.wikipedia.org/wiki/X_Prize_Foundation
[19] https://en.wikipedia.org/wiki/Ansari_X_Prize#Contestants

The approach has been around for a while. In 1927, Charles Lindberg flew the Spirit of St. Louis non-stop from New York to Paris to claim the $25,000 Orteig Prize.[20]

- **Sponsorship and Support**: Provide resources to people whose goals are aligned with things that matter to the organization, but don't get too involved in the details.

> NASA applies this approach with their Early-Stage Innovations (ESI) program. The goal of ESI is to "accelerate the development of groundbreaking, high-risk/high-payoff space technologies to support the future space science and exploration needs of NASA."[21] Each year, they publish a list of technologies they would like to explore, and they fund companies who make promising proposals. If the technologies progress according to the Technology Readiness Levels, additional funds can be granted.[22]

> SpaceX applies this approach internally by having a clear focus on reducing the cost of getting a payload into Low Earth Orbit. If a SpaceX engineer wants to pursue an idea that can lower cost to orbit, if SpaceX can afford it, it will get funded.[23]

In battle, control is still essential, but a more resilient and flexible approach to command is required.

Mission Command assumes the environment is chaotic, literally a battlefield, so both responsiveness and resiliency are essential to success. Instructions are not simply, "take the hill." The instructions include how taking the hill fits into the larger strategy. This deeper why is called "commander's intent."

The unit will do their best to take the hill, but if they see they cannot achieve that goal, they will strive do the next best thing. Or, if they see an opportunity to achieve a better result, they can do that too. And they can call for help if they need it.

---

[20] https://en.wikipedia.org/wiki/Orteig_Prize

[21] https://www.nasa.gov/directorates/spacetech/strg/early-stage-innovations-esi

[22] https://en.wikipedia.org/wiki/Technology_readiness_level

[23] Joe Justice on Product Ownership at SpaceX and Tesla - Product Owner Festival Opening Keynote, https://youtu.be/7h9YFRVetcQ

To achieve resilience, every soldier is trained to see the bigger picture and to be able to take command of their unit if necessary. Rank ensures an understanding of who is in command and any conflict can be resolved quickly. Leadership training is not just for officers, but for everybody.

In nature, we see the flock of birds. Any bird in the flock can lead the flock and the flock holds together. Can your organization say that anyone in the organization can step up and take command of a situation when the need arises?

The Scrum Framework is a civilian implementation of mission command. This approach empowers self-organization among teams. A frequent impediment to a successful Agile transformation with Scrum is the disbelief on the part of leadership that ordinary staff are capable of taking the necessary responsibility or are willing to do so. In short, this lack of trust and alignment prevents organizations from moving forward.

IV. THE IMPORTANCE OF ALIGNMENT

Many companies struggle with alignment. True alignment depends not just on knowing what to do, but on knowing, agreeing, and caring about the why of what you are doing. Alignment requires trust, and as we saw in Chapter 6, trust requires empathy.

Without agreement on purpose—or as we call it, What Really Matters—goals can change whenever particular stakeholders gain or lose influence. If priorities change every few weeks or as a reaction to stakeholder intervention, the course becomes unpredictable. It is difficult for an organization to achieve long-term goals under these conditions. The goals change faster than teams can achieve them.

A practitioner of the Personal Agility System doesn't just know what they are doing, they understand why they are doing it. How does Personal Agility apply beyond a single individual? Imagine your organization if everybody understood why they were doing what they were doing, and all the stakeholders agreed on the key initiatives and their importance!

Leadership is "a process of social influence in which a person can enlist the aid and support of others in the accomplishment of a common task,"[24] or, more fundamentally, motivating the people around you to follow your direction.

When we look at successful endeavors, we see that cadence, clarity of purpose and simple rules of engagement are key to this success. Alignment is a fancy word for "everyone understands what we are doing and why we are doing it." Alignment is the holy grail of large organizations. "If we could only get everyone on the same page, pulling in the same direction…"

Rules of engagement cause people to act in ways that support the overall goals.

If the people doing the work are engaged, they will go the extra mile to achieve great things. When people feel aligned to a greater purpose, this increases their motivation. When they have autonomy, this leads to self-fulfillment. Many people believe autonomy causes chaos. How can you achieve both alignment and autonomy at the same time? Through clarity of purpose.

Often, our job as leaders is to understand the needs of our stakeholders, or even help them to better understand their needs. How do you help your stakeholders achieve clarity of purpose or even identify a common purpose that they can all agree on?

In this chapter, we will give you tools to achieve clarity of purpose. Given that an organization has multiple objectives, we'll share tools that will help you balance those against each other so your organization can achieve high performance instead of overloading itself. When you create alignment, you can be the Agile leader that others want to follow.

V. CLARITY OF PURPOSE

Fifty-some years ago, mankind first set foot on the Moon. Two astronauts did the walking, and one person spoke the first words. But the effort was massive. It was probably the largest mobilization of a country's resources for a peaceful purpose up until that point in history. Between NASA, the military, other government agencies and civilian contractors, over 400,000 people were involved in the Apollo program.

---

[24] https://en.wikipedia.org/wiki/Leadership, extracted 26 Feb 2020

How do you organize so many people to achieve such a seemingly impossible goal in less than a decade?

In 2019, Peter Stevens attended Starmus V in Zurich, Switzerland, which celebrated the 50th anniversary of the first Apollo landing. There, he listened to stories told by astronauts, mission controllers, and administrators of the US and Soviet programs to understand how the Space Race between the USA and the USSR was won.

The Soviets entered the race with a three-year lead, but it turned out that the Americans held many of the defining advantages. President John F. Kennedy did not commit America to going to the Moon. He asked America to commit to sending a man to the moon and bringing him safely back to Earth. There was one program with one goal, not several programs competing primarily with each other. Nor was the mission overloaded with unrelated objectives. Leadership was 100% committed and the rest of the country followed suit.

Everybody involved in the program knew two things:

1. "We are going to the moon."

2. "It is not going to fail because of me."

These two statements told everybody everything they needed to know about their role in the program. Clarity of purpose enabled good decision-making at all levels of the organization.

Everybody understood what really mattered: having a successful mission. There was one goal and a clear purpose.

Even the vendors weren't just delivering goods to a program; they were essential partners. For example, the seamstresses at ILC Dover knew how important their jobs were. "They may have had the most important job of all, frankly," said Basil Hero, author of the Apollo account *The Mission of a Lifetime*. As Neil Armstrong said, "Those space suits were mini spacecrafts. You were one pin prick away from death. If those suits failed, that was it. You were done."

Organizations today often present a very different picture. Instead of one mission and one goal, organizations (and the individuals in them) have many goals, many managers, many things to do in parallel, and constantly changing priorities about what people should work on. It's difficult to care about or take responsibility for anything because the priority could change tomorrow, and that passion and energy will have been wasted.

This leads to people disengaging. They do what they must do to keep their jobs, but anything beyond that is wasted energy.

How many people know how their work ties into the goals of the company or the satisfaction of their customers? Do they know what initiatives are important to the company, why they are important, or how many people are focused on achieving the goal of each initiative? We saw in Chapter Four that multitasking kills performance, but if the company has many goals to achieve, how can they achieve them without excessive multitasking?

Personal Agility offers a way out. As always, the key question is, What Really Matters?

VI. GUIDE BEHAVIOR TO HARNESS EMERGENCE

> *"Leadership is unlocking people's potential to become better."*
> **Bill Bradley**

There is more to leading an organization than setting a destination. Projects require the collaboration of many people, potentially hundreds or even thousands. How do you keep moving in the same direction? How do you ensure alignment?

You can take a group of people, give them a yellow jersey, and call them a football team. Does that make them a team? Only when they practice together, work together, develop a system of play together, and learn to trust each other, do they become a team. Some teams win more often than others. Even though a stranger to the game may just see people in jerseys, there is something about how they play together that makes them special.

Emergence occurs when individuals interact with each other to make something bigger than themselves. One example is the sports team, but this *coming together to make something bigger than yourself* appears to be a fundamental organizing principle of the universe.

Take a flock of birds. Scientists studied the motion of flying birds to create realistic simulations of their behavior. It turns out the birds only need three simple rules to hold together as a flock: 1) Fly in the same direction as the birds around you, 2) fly close to the birds around you, and 3) don't get too close to the birds around you. If the birds don't follow these rules, the flock doesn't hold together. When the birds do follow the rules, you get a flock.

Now, let's take a closer look at the Apollo project. Everyone knew the goal: to bring a man to the moon and return him safely to earth before the decade was out. There was something else everyone knew: "It's not going to fail because of me." This simple sentence enabled all 400,000 people from the government, the military, and the civilian economy to focus on and do the right thing.

Rules of engagement guide the behavior of individuals, which in turn changes the character and culture of their teams and organizations. For example, when a group of top leaders come together to determine the vision moving forward, there are often people with strong opinions in the room who are also good at debating. It may be difficult to arrive at a conclusion.

Let's revisit Michael's story at Vivior. To present and discuss new ideas effectively, during their workshop, they agreed to the simple rules we presented in Chapter 5, Business Coaching: Listen before you talk; ask before you tell; ask clarifying questions and let people finish their sentences. So rather than listen to debate or score the next point, they listened for understanding and asked constructive questions to better understand the situation. At the end of the day, all the leaders had learned a lot about the possible courses of action. The choice was relatively clear. They voted and everybody accepted the decision.

The dialogue approach upon which Personal Agility is based enables you to surface valuable information to make better decisions without unnecessary conflict. Ask before you talk and listen before you tell are fundamental patterns of Personal Agility. This communication defines the interactions between the individuals around you. It shapes your culture so that strong and flexible organizations can emerge.

How do you create these simple rules of engagement? Step one is to clarify the goal for everyone involved. Step two is to identify behavior that will lead to the right conclusion, like these examples from Chapter 5:

- Ask clarifying questions

- Listen for understanding

- Ask before you tell

- Ask "How does this serve our purpose?"

Rules of engagement can replace a command and control-based culture. Let's take expense reports as an example. Traditionally, somebody reviews and approves expense reports to ensure that the company's money is being spent properly. This is often accompanied by a list of rules and policies covering what is allowed and what is not. How can you achieve the same goal by guiding behavior? Netflix addressed this problem with a simple "no rules" rule:

"Spend company money as if it were your own."[25]

This simple guideline was intended to ensure that company money is well spent. They later discovered that this was too vague as people had very divergent ideas about how to spend their own money. Did they return to expense reports? No. They updated the rule: Act in Netflix's Best Interest. Add transparency—e.g., publish your expenses on an in-house blog—and the goals of the traditional review-and-approve process have been achieved. Netflix called this process of creating more visibility "sunshining it" and applied it to more than just expense reports.

VII. ACHIEVING AUTONOMY AND ALIGNMENT

> *"Control leads to compliance; autonomy leads to engagement."*
>
> **Daniel H. Pink**

Daniel Pink wrote in his book *Drive* that the prerequisites for motivation are autonomy, mastery, and purpose. Autonomy is the need to direct your own life and work. Mastery is the desire to develop your skills. Purpose is the deeper why behind what you are doing. When people believe they are working toward something larger and more important than themselves, they are often more productive and engaged.

It is rare to see a person or organization focusing on just one thing. Musicians, Olympians, professional sports teams, and bodybuilders are all examples of the excellence that can be achieved through a singular focus, but we rarely see this type of dedication in organizations.

---

[25] No Rules Rules, https://itsyourturnblog.com/no-rules-rules-e23c40ebc0bf

The Apollo program was very clear, but the Space Race was just one part of the larger US government. Companies today usually don't have just one goal either. How do you achieve alignment and autonomy while pursuing multiple goals? And how many goals can a company effectively pursue simultaneously?

The current situation we often see in organizations is that people are typically working on multiple concurrent projects. Joe's manager gets a request like: "I need someone with Joe's skills" (and Joe may be the only person with those skills). "You can have Joe, but I need him to spend 30% of his time and resources supporting his current project." And so it goes. The people in the company get spread more and more thinly across multiple initiatives until it is not uncommon for people to be working on five or more projects at once. Everybody is busy, but actual progress slows to a crawl.

Often, companies lack the tools to see and understand the impact of this overload, and leadership is unable to react appropriately.

Typical symptoms of excessive multitasking include projects that miss deadlines and compromise quality, which in turn causes defects and customer complaints that must eventually be addressed. As a result, team morale goes down. How could clarity on What Really Matters change this? Let's use the hypothetical Sample.com as an example.

Imagine a Priorities Map for the whole company. Sample.com's leadership agrees on which initiatives would, if successful, bring the most benefit and communicates that list to the whole company. Each initiative is a card in the What Really Matters column. These cards are ranked by strong prioritization. The topmost card is more important than the second card, which is more important than the third, etc.

Let's assume Sample.com has the following initiatives, and that this list is sorted by potential value (or other measure of importance):

- Expand to the mobile market

- Bring new product X to market

- Bring new product Y to market

- Upgrade system and network infrastructure

- Upgrade existing product S to defend its market position

- etc.

Why is Mobile the most important initiative? This needs to be both clear and agreed upon by the key stakeholders.

How do you avoid spreading your people and resources too thin? Let's add a simple rule to ensure the company focuses on the right things: A high priority initiative never waits on or shares people or resources with a lower priority initiative. Everyone can understand and apply this constraint to make the right decisions about how to allocate their time, people, and other resources.

Here's how it could work. Let's assume that Sample.com has ten teams, named Team A, Team B, Team C, etc. through Team J. Which teams are needed for the mobile market expansion? Teams A, C, and D. Mobile gets those teams. Which teams are needed to bring Product X to market? Teams B, E, and F. No conflicts arise, so Product X gets the teams. Which teams are needed for bringing Product Y to market? Teams D, G and H.

Uh oh. Both initiatives Mobile and Product Y need Team D. What happens next? One approach would have Team D divide their time between the two efforts. Or the leadership might arm-wrestle over the teams and, depending on who is winning at the time, the priorities and focus might shift from month to month or even week to week.

As we saw in the chapter on multitasking, either approach slows down both initiatives, while increasing the cost, time-to-market, and probability of failure. The agreement to focus first on the top priority initiative enables a clear decision to work on the mobile market.

What happens to Product Y? Either the company finds another team to substitute for Team D—maybe Team J could also do the job—or product Y waits until all the necessary teams are available.

This simple approach limits the number of initiatives the company has in progress. It ensures that the company a) is always focused on the top priority initiatives with the necessary energy, people, and resources, and b) only takes on as many initiatives as it can effectively handle.

Limiting Work in Progress (WIP) is a widely used practice to combat excessive multitasking. This is a core principle of the Kanban method. The approach outlined here uses alignment on priorities and available capacity to limit the WIP at the organizational level.

Some teams might not be assigned permanently to any one initiative, for example IT Support. By understanding the company's priorities, they can ask themselves, how can we best support the Mobile initiative? A shared understanding of What Really Matters enables anybody in the company to align with the goals of the organization.

Spotify pioneered a similar approach. They call the What Really Matters column "bets," they focus on these high priority bets, and they review these priorities at regular intervals.[26]

The key here is to have a WIP Limit on initiatives. The high priority bets get the focus while other initiatives wait. It's a simple prioritization algorithm. If two bets need a person or resources, the higher priority bet gets them. A lower priority cannot take people or resources away from the higher priority initiative.

These clear priorities allow people to focus on these top initiatives with little interruption.

How does Sample.com achieve alignment and autonomy? By communicating the What Really Matters column so everybody knows what is important and why it is important. By understanding why, each member of the company can make decisions that support the key goals of the company. This is alignment.

The What Really Matters column is an enumeration of purpose. You create alignment by sharing What Really Matters. People can make decisions about what to do and how to do it. This delegation of responsibility in the context of a purpose enables people to decide what the right thing is to do. This is aligned autonomy.

When you start, you may discover that What Really Matters is poorly understood, or that there are many different visions coming from various parts of the organization. It is important to figure out what your stakeholders really want and build consensus around this vision.

---

[26] https://blog.crisp.se/2016/06/08/henrikkniberg/spotify-rhythm

VIII. ALIGNING WITH STAKEHOLDERS

> *"The key to successful leadership today*
> *is influence, not authority."*
>
> **Kenneth Blanchard**

Remember Hugo Lourenco from Chapter One, the entrepreneur based in Lisbon, Portugal? Seven months after starting with PAS and shedding many non-productive activities, Hugo had taken an engagement as an external Agile Coach and Project Leader for a large consulting company.

"I was taking over the leadership of a project that was to deliver a solution to the customers of my client. The situation was challenging, because there was the client, and the client's clients, each with their own set of stakeholders and potentially conflicting interests. How do you work with stakeholders in such a complex environment?

"I needed to figure out what the customers were really looking for. I had a client who wanted to use Agile practices for a project for their customers, but the situation was very complex. I wanted to build trust and alignment. The idea was to understand the situation, the stakeholders, and the real issues so I could build trust and so the stakeholders would understand what we were trying to achieve.

"I interviewed all my key stakeholders, both at my client and at their customers, using the PAS Stakeholder Canvas to understand the situation.

"During the conversations, the questions of the Stakeholder Canvas triggered strong feelings of happiness in people. They told me, 'I have worked on several projects, but no one has ever asked me about success or failure.' I was alone with the people, I took time with them, which people don't usually do. People almost had tears in their eyes because people never seem to care about them or their contribution. No one in the company had done this before.

"By the content of the answers, I was also able to identify which people belonged in the project, but also who shouldn't belong in the project. Some people would take an open-ended question and turn it into a closed-ended question. It became clear that some people just didn't have a clue.

"I engaged with and energized the people who belonged in the project."

How do you figure out What Really Matters to your stakeholders?

The classic business definition of a stakeholder is anyone who has an interest in what you're doing on a project. In the real world, a stakeholder is anyone who can helicopter into your project and completely toss out all the assumptions, plans and results prepared to date. For this reason, stakeholder management is essential to successful endeavors.

In our experience, stakeholder management is easiest when you and your stakeholders trust each other. When your stakeholders know that you are listening to them and understand them, they can have confidence that you can represent their interests moving forward.

How do you build trust with a stakeholder? Connect with them as a person and ensure you are on the same page. This can help with understanding the problem you're trying to solve, establishing a stronger relationship, and most importantly, understanding the official and hidden agendas and motivations of the people involved.

The first step is to listen to what your stakeholders have to say. Listen for understanding, not to debate or convince. We often enter conversations wanting others to see our point of view. Ironically, the best way to get stakeholders to listen to you is for you to listen to them.

We created the PAS Stakeholder Canvas to help you start a relationship with new customers or stakeholders. The Stakeholder Canvas provides a coaching approach to working with stakeholders. It's both a script for asking useful questions and a template for recording the answers. Listen to your stakeholders. *Really* listen to them. By understanding What Really Matters to them, you establish your credibility as a trusted partner.

You can get an idea of how it works by taking a look at the excerpt on page 126. To really use it, it's best to download the original from the Personal Agility Institute website.[27]

---

[27] http://www.PersonalAgilityInstitute.org/dashboard (Registration required)

Use this canvas to guide your conversations with your stakeholders about your collaboration or the project you are working on. We suggest planning an interview of around 30 to 60 minutes.

The first column relates to who the stakeholder is, their main goals and objectives, and ultimately What Really Matters to them. The second column relates to their motivations. Risks and fears apply to emotional motivations looking forward, and frustrations apply to emotional motivations looking backward. Challenges and impediments are about the actual problem to be solved or solution to be delivered, not about emotions. The third column focuses on the desired outcome.

While the columns are organized by theme, we recommend asking the questions in the numbered order—although you could jump around a bit if it feels appropriate. Note that we don't ask the What Really Matters question until later in the order of questions. Going through the thought process of the other questions first can help build context.

The Personal Agility System™

PAS STAKEHOLDER CANVAS

To figure out what really matters to your stakeholders, address the topics in order. Sample questions are for your inspiration.

1. Stakeholder	2. Main Goals	8. What Really Matters?
Note and if necessary, confirm the person's Name, Function, Contact Details	What is your goal or purpose in this relationship? How will information be used?	At the end of the day, what is most essential? Have I missed something important? Is there anything else?
3. Challenges	**4. Risks, Concerns, Fears**	**5. Frustrations**
What is making this hard to do? What are the main challenges to achieving these goals or desired outcome? What are the technical or functional issues?	What could go wrong? What are you afraid of? What gives you stomach aches? What make you lose sleep at night?	Where do you see cooperation issues? What causes you to bang your head against the wall? What recurring problems keep coming up?
6. Definition of Awesome	**7. Support**	**9. Next Steps**
Imagine that a miracle happens overnight... What is the best possible outcome?	How can I support you? What issues can I help you address? Who can help? Who else shares your perspective?	Here is what to expect next... What are possible next steps? What would helpful at this point?

Coaching questions can be helpful to elicit better, more complete answers, i.e. "Is there anything else?" or "Let me read this back to you; have I understood you correctly?" Sometimes it is helpful to vary how you formulate the question so that it resonates better with your interview partner.

Your overall goal is to design your activities around helping your stakeholders master their challenges, reduce their fears, and eliminate their frustrations, to achieve their optimal outcome. Your immediate goal is to demonstrate that you understand them and their desired outcome, and that you are focused on making it happen.

You may find it useful after the interviewee has answered each question to answer the questions yourself. This helps the interviewee understand you as well as you understand them.

You can use the following script to lead a stakeholder through the interview:

SAMPLE SCRIPT

As you know, we are working on the "Xyzzy" initiative. Beyond that, my goal is to create an effective partnership between us, so that we can work together effectively with minimal friction. I want to focus on doing great things for you and your customers. To that end, I would like to understand you, your goals, and your perspective.

1. **Stakeholder** - Confirm the person's name and contact information.

2. **Main Goals or Objectives** - "What do you want to achieve through this project or collaboration?"

3. **Challenges and Impediments** - "What are the main challenges standing between you and achieving your goals or desired outcome?"

4. **Risks, Concerns, Fears** - "What concerns you about achieving your goals?"

5. **Frustrations** - "What problems keep coming up that cause you to bang your head against the wall?"

6. **Definition of Awesome** - "If I could snap my fingers and all your wishes came true on this project, what would that look like?"

7. **Support** - "How can I/we support you to make this come true?"

8. **What Really Matters**? - "From what I have heard you say, when push comes to shove, these three points are the most essential... Have I understood you correctly?" Summarize and validate your understanding of the stakeholder's key concerns. If you are correct, you have an agreement about What Really Matters.

9. **What's next**? - What is the next thing that you need to do for this stakeholder (follow-up)?

WHAT TO DO WITH THE RESULTS?

When dealing with many stakeholders, look for patterns, similarities, and glaring differences. Use the information gleaned to guide your collaboration and the definition of your project goal.

A stakeholder (or the entity they represent) could become a column in your Forces Map. The top card would contain:

- A picture or icon of the stakeholder
- Their perspective on What Really Matters
- Their definition of awesome

Individual cards might correspond to specific goals, features, or tasks to help them achieve their "awesome" state.

TIPS FOR INTERVIEWING STAKEHOLDERS

By understanding who your stakeholders are, what their goals are, what their challenges, fears and frustrations are, as well as the optimal outcome and what help they need, you get a complete understanding of the situation at hand and can constructively discuss how to move forward.

Ask them these questions and listen to what they are saying. Take notes and read what they said back to them. Ask, "Is there anything else? Have I heard you correctly?" This gives both parties confirmation that you have heard and understood the whole problem.

When can you share your perspective? After you have listened to them and they have confirmed that you have understood them correctly and completely, you can bring in your inputs: "In my experience, I have found that this can also be an issue..." "Oh, that's interesting. What can we do about this?" "Let's have a conversation about that..."

There are a couple of things to avoid: selling, debating, or arguing. These activities might happen later, but they do not build trust. If you find yourself in a conversation where you are interrupting each other or trying to get the other person to listen, then you need to listen more and talk less!

Building trust is not about convincing someone else to follow a particular direction or selling them on an idea (though trust building can be a selling technique). It's about listening for understanding. Listening for understanding provides opportunities for deep learning and connection. Typically, if you don't listen to others, they won't listen to you. When you stop to listen, that's when you really begin to connect.

At this point, you can formulate your purpose, enable autonomy while maintaining alignment, and understand your stakeholders on a deeper level, which in turn will help you guide them toward figuring out what matters to them and the organization.

CHAPTER 8.
EXECUTIVE AGILITY:
HOW TO BE AN AGILE LEADER

While you've already learned about effective leadership, this chapter will explore the unity between effective leadership and the concept of Agility.

You will begin by learning what it means to truly be an Agile executive, and how this enables greater adaptability in the face of increasingly fast-moving, complex markets.

You will then learn how to extend these concepts of Agility across your teams and departments, with the goal of creating an Agile organization. You will also explore different ways of extending Agility to your customers and clients, and where to begin so you can achieve results as soon as possible.

> *"Morale is a multiplier for velocity."*
>
> **Joe Justice**

I. CASE STUDY:
BUILDING A CULTURE OF EMPOWERMENT

Ben Sever is CEO of eRemede, a rapidly growing Health Tech company in Tampa, Florida. Their focus is enterprise level services that are compliant with the Health Insurance Portability and Accountability Act (HIPAA).

The goal was to quickly establish the company as a player in a new line of business, despite the complexity and compliance requirements of health care solutions. The whole team had already been through Certified ScrumMaster® training and were working more productively thanks to the training.

"My biggest challenge was the inability to let go and delegate large projects and deliverables to others. As a CEO, I was underutilizing my team and taking on too much. I wasn't effectively delegating to my leadership team, which led to me not working at a sustainable pace."

> *"We reached our desired valuation in half the time."*
>
> **Ben Sever, CEO eRemede, Tampa, Florida**

"Our original roadmap was to be worth $35 million after three years. We shortened the timeline to reach our desired valuation in half the time."

Ben and his executive team learned PAS together with training and coaching led by Maria. They took advantage of the full palette of the Personal Agility System, including identifying What Really Matters, the PAS Forces Map, PAS Priorities Map and Breadcrumb Trail, and the Celebrate and Choose event.

"The Personal Agility System allowed the entire executive team to better empathize with each other. Because we're empowering each other's personal lives, we could motivate each other, understand each other, and trust each other. I could stop taking on everything myself, and our performance as an organization really accelerated.

"As our team grew and our clientele became Enterprise, we realized that it was essential to better understand our people. When leaders take the time to reflect on What Really Matters and to understand the motivation of the people they work with every day, they can optimize the individual connections that lead to increased alignment.

"Before, my executive team knew Scrum and they knew Agile as a concept, but Personal Agility allowed them to embody, embrace, and live optimally, resulting in an organic co-creation of self-organizing teams and optimized performance.

"Today, we are an Agile organization. Agility enables us to be successful in today's complex world. My role as CEO has evolved into being a Chief Empowerment Officer."

II. HOW TO BE AN AGILE EXECUTIVE

What does it mean to be Agile? In 2001, seventeen leading software developers formulated the Agile Manifesto and started a movement which has gained attention far beyond the world of software.

> *"We are uncovering better ways of developing software*
> *by doing it and helping others do it...*
> *Our highest priority is to satisfy the customer*
> *through early and continuous delivery of valuable software."*
>
> **The Manifesto for Agile Software Development**[28]

Let's look at this beyond the context of software. Agility is about "uncovering better ways;" there is no one "best" practice, only the search for a better practice. It's about "doing it and helping others to do it"—collaboration. And finally, "our highest priority" is about purpose. Agility is about learning, collaboration, and clarity of purpose.

Executives lead people and organizations in a complex world. Agile executives uncover better ways of running their companies, by doing it and helping each other to do the same. They strive to optimize their company's culture and structure to produce value sooner.

An Agile executive:

- Knows What Really Matters to the organization,
- Learns through dialogue and collaboration,
- Applies cadence for effective decision-making and holding focus,
- Shapes the culture of the organization by guiding emergence, and
- Recognizes when it's better to stay out of the way.

These simple tools enable the Agile executive to create a more responsive enterprise. They can maximize their own impact, achieve genuine alignment, and focus and structure their organization. By ensuring the rapid flow of information, they can resolve challenges and issues quickly and effectively to activate their organization's full potential.

Executive Agility enables companies to be more responsive, more flexible, more effective, and able to create more value faster. This makes them more successful in the market.

An Agile company learns quickly and effectively, collaborates willingly, and knows why they do what they do. So does an Agile executive. Your positive attitude toward

---

[28] https://agilemanifesto.org

collaboration, continuous learning, and continuous improvement empowers you and makes you more effective.

III. HOW TO CREATE AN AGILE ORGANIZATION?

> *"An Agile Transformation restructures the company to optimize for speed and value production."*
>
> **Joe Justice**

Today, many companies want to be more Agile so they can build better products, respond better to changing market conditions, get to market faster, have higher performing teams, and ultimately increase market share and earn more money. The leaders tell their IT people (and more recently their businesspeople) to "be Agile." Use this tool, apply that framework. But neither the tool nor the framework makes you Agile. These were developed by people who are Agile so they could do their work better. You can invite people to be Agile but telling people to be Agile is almost always counterproductive.

The most successful patterns we have seen are when leaders embrace Agility; the spread isn't purely top-down nor bottom-up but is best described as viral. Top leaders and other influencers "dance the dance" and the rest of the organization follows.

Leading by example is key.

"All of our projects are managed somewhere," explains Walter Stulzer, Executive Director of Futureworks in Zurich. "Agile projects have task boards, classic projects have traditional tools. But what about my work? What about the things I can't delegate? I manage the things that aren't projects with Personal Agility."

Klemens Buob, CFO of Sisag AG, started their Agile transition by putting a Priorities Map on the wall in his office. There, he managed his own work. Every time someone came to visit him, be that an employee, a supplier, or a customer, they would see this new thing on the wall and ask questions. By explaining how he managed his own work, he was able to share ideas as well as his passion and energy. He gave people implicit permission and inspiration to try the approach for themselves.

When they started using a software tool to visualize their work, it spread like wildfire across the company. Suddenly, the Agile way of working wasn't strange, it was normal, and the company was able to move forward quickly.

When Sisag started applying other Agile techniques, like Scrum, they were natural extensions of Personal Agility. Everyone understood easily why it was beneficial to themselves or the company. "The most important thing is that every few weeks, we get to consider what brings value and what doesn't. We can then choose to do those things that bring value," explained Erich Megert, Chief Marketing Officer of the Board at Sisag AG.

Embracing Agility yourself sets the tone for your entire organization. As Agile leadership coach Michael Sahota says, "You have to put the oxygen mask on yourself first before you can help others." Uncover better ways of doing what you do by doing it and helping others do it. Focus on continuous learning and improvement and empower your teams.

While taking Agility to the rest of your organization is beyond the scope of this book, we'd like to share a few pointers to increase your chances of success.

The purpose of an Agile transformation is to enable the company to innovate more effectively and produce tangible results sooner. It's not just making a few changes in the IT department.

Agile transformation entails rethinking the relationship between leadership, management, and operational staff. Traditionally, leadership provides direction, management prevents chaos by keeping things under control, and the other employees do the work of the business. In an Agile organization, the Agile teams can organize themselves to prevent chaos, so much less management is necessary and a more collaborative relationship between leadership and the teams becomes essential.

Personal Agility has given you tools, techniques and thought models to navigate, prioritize, solve problems collaboratively, and build alignment among your stakeholders. As you move forward, you can apply them in your organization to support key objectives of the transformation:

- **Alignment**: create alignment through listening and collaborative problem-solving. Disseminate alignment with Priorities Maps and clear statements of What Really Matters.

- **Responsiveness**: the "Celebrate and Choose" event, coupled with a Priorities Map, is a scalable pattern for identifying and prioritizing work.

- **Culture**: Powerful questions are applicable in nearly any context to make sense of a challenge, identify causes and possible solutions, and select a course of action. Simple guidelines like "ask before you tell" or "spend company money like your own" make it easy for people to do the right thing.

The most visible change that occurs during an Agile transformation is the evolution of the organizational structure. Conway's law postulates that the architecture of a product reflects the structure of the organization that produced it. You can turn that around by first creating cross-functional teams to design your products, then scaling the organization around the design of those products. The result is a product organization that is optimized for speed and efficiency.

IV. HOW TO EXTEND AGILITY TO YOUR CUSTOMERS

Let's revisit Vivior, whose turnaround we presented in Chapter Six. Andreas Kelch is the Head of Sales and Marketing for Vision Care in Europe. They developed a new technology and a new product for opticians. By mid-2021 they had successfully acquired 90 customers, mainly in Switzerland and Germany. However, the integration of Vivior into the business processes of opticians proved to be a challenge.

Vivior applied the same techniques to build alignment with their customers that they used to build alignment among the leadership. The PAS Stakeholder Canvas played a key role in establishing a constructive relationship with their customers that was trust-based, goal-oriented, and quantitatively measurable.

Andreas explained, "Business processes vary from optician to optician. We wanted to understand our customers even better, so we developed a new customer management process. We want the optician to recognize the added value of Vivior to their business.

"As the pandemic subsided, our customers experienced a large increase in business which kept them busy processing orders. They were also confronted with labor shortages and other constraints, so there was little time available to deal with new technologies such as ours.

"We saw potential in strengthening our personal customer relationships."

For a startup, the most important goal is traction. "Within our new customer management process, we created an on-boarding process with defined steps to manage and monitor our own success.

"Once the customer agrees to buy our product, we meet and interview them using the PAS Stakeholder Canvas. We had tailored the questions to our context. The canvas asks questions about goals and challenges and the conversation offers us an opportunity to share our insights. Based on their goals, they define their 'customer commitment'—what they need to do to be successful.

"The customers appreciated that we offered this consultancy service to them—that we did not leave them alone and that we cared about their success. The interviews were well received as they were perceived as a service to get their problems solved.

"Every active customer now has an action plan with an integrated commitment to concrete usage goals. We can make visible to everyone involved how important the technology is to them. The commitment is important both to the customer and to us. The customer sees the value they get from the product and how to differentiate themselves in a competitive market. We can define and meet our scaling goals."

The techniques of understanding your customer are the same as for understanding your stakeholders: Ask them powerful questions to understand What Really Matters to them. Pay particular attention to their challenges, fears, and frustrations. Identify their definition of awesome, and how your definition of awesome aligns with theirs. Build consensus around What Really Matters, then use their definition of awesome to identify goals that are in both your interests.

V. ACHIEVING RESULTS

Remember Walter Stulzer from the Introduction? The way they had operated in years past was not getting them where they needed to go. Introducing focus, clarity, and tangible results in cadence made the difference.

As you begin your journey, start where it is easiest. You can choose to apply Personal Agility to your own life or work without asking anyone's permission. Each step leads to the next, and before you know it, your actions will be aligned, and you will be systematically achieving your goals.

In the next chapter, we will review what you have learned so you can apply it in your life and organization.

CHAPTER 9.
REVIEW AND NEXT STEPS

W e've shared many examples of how The Personal Agility System can be used across different situations. We've shared some strategies for getting started. The next step is yours.

Let's review what you have learned.

In Part One, we began at the individual level: how can you be more effective in your life and work?

In Chapter One, we presented an overview of PAS so you could see how the pieces fit together. PAS enables you to organize yourself and lead others.

In Chapter Two, we presented case studies that represented potentially millions of people who could improve their lives with Personal Agility. As Personal Agility becomes widespread, it could have a huge impact on our quality of life.

In Chapter Three, you learned how to clarify What Really Matters, so you could align what you do with What Really Matters to you.

In Chapter Four, you learned about handling interruptions and distractions so you could be more effective at achieving long-term goals. You also learned that multitasking is bad for performance and procrastination is trying to tell you something.

In Part Two we shifted the focus from personal to the organization. How can your organization be more responsive, more effective, and more Agile?

In Chapter Five, you learned why coaching is the new management, and how to apply powerful questions and interactions to solve problems and activate the intelligence in your teams.

In Chapter Six, you learned how to build trust and empathy to create alignment with your stakeholders.

In Chapter Seven, you learned new approaches to achieving decisiveness and holding focus in the organization. You discovered why emergence is the missing link in leadership, and explored tools to identify consensus and build alignment among your stakeholders, managers, customers, and colleagues.

In Chapter Eight, you learned to apply this in your role as a leader. We showed the impact of applying these principles with your leadership team, board of directors, and other stakeholders.

So, what are your next steps?

The easiest place to start is usually yourself. Once you have discovered the power of Personal Agility, you can lead by example.

Here are some places to start:

1. Manage Yourself for Maximum Impact

If you haven't started using the Priorities Map yet, now is a great time to start. Find someone in the community—either a Recognized Ambassador, Trainer, or Coach—to get you started. This will help you identify and unlock your purpose in life and business.

Getting the right things done depends on your ability to set the right priorities, work according to priority, and complete tasks in cadence. Practice these skills in your own life first. Then, when the time comes to apply these skills at work, you will be able to take a leadership role in your company's Agile transformation.

You can lead by example because these techniques will already be second nature to you.

2. Explore the Potential of Powerful Questions

Now is the time to introduce powerful questions to your vocabulary. Use the canvases and question catalogs made available by the Personal Agility Institute. When you can activate the intelligence in your organization, you become the go-to person for solving your organization's toughest challenges. This will help you both move towards achieving your purpose and assist in creating alignment with your teams.

Powerful questions are the management tool of the 21st century. Rather than telling people what to do, you invite people to think about the big picture and the problem at hand. By inviting your staff to think, you empower them to take responsibility. You are laying the foundations of a responsive organization.

3. Harness Emergence

Start culture hacking in your organization with small experiments and working agreements. Promote simple rules of engagement to encourage people to interact effectively and do the right things. Ask clarifying questions. Emergence will naturally create alignment among teams. Transforming your own practices via Agility will in turn propagate the transformation throughout your organization.

4. Harness Clarity of Purpose

Agreement on What Really Matters creates clarity of purpose, which makes decision-making easier. Interview your stakeholders with the Stakeholder Canvas to build alignment, which is the basis for focus and decisive action. When you have alignment, your initiatives can move forward without political resistance.

5. Continue the Conversation

Join our community at www.PersonalAgilityInstitute.org/join

You'll get access to:

- Guide to Personal Agility
- PAS Priorities Map & Breadcrumb Trail Template
- PAS Forces Map Template
- PAS Alignment Compass Template
- PAS Stakeholder Canvas
- PAS Problem Solving Canvas
- PAS Powerful Question Catalogues
- PAS Knowledge Base and Case Studies
- Additional tools as they become available

We have only begun to explore the potential of Personal Agility. We would like to work with people and organizations who share our goals and vision.

Reach out to us at www.PersonalAgilityInstitute.org/contact to embark on this journey and begin making your vision a reality.

THANK YOU FOR READING!

Join the community to share your thoughts and ask us questions!

Join the Community!

https://PersonalAgilityInstitute.org/join

(register to contribute)

We look forward to continuing this journey with you.

    Sincerely,
    Peter and Maria

DISCOVER THE PERSONAL AGILITY SYSTEM FROM THE EXPERTS!

For leaders, managers, coaches, consultants, and project leaders who want better alignment with themselves and more impact at work.

Would you like to:

- Find a balance between life and work?

- Develop your coaching skills?

- Deliver on your commitments?

- Be more efficient and have more impact at work?

- Understand what employers, customers and stakeholders really want from you?

Our worldwide network of trainers and ambassadors can help you do more of What Really Matters and become the person you want to be!

LEARN TO APPLY PERSONAL AGILITY, THE GPS NAVIGATOR FOR YOUR LIFE AND PROJECTS!

> *"I was able to gain insight not only into a system and approach that will help me finish my own book, but also significant insight into myself. The Personal Agility approach has filled my sails with inspiration and well-founded confidence."*
>
> **David Barg, former guest conductor**
> **NY Philharmonic Education Department**

ABOUT THE AUTHORS

PETER B. STEVENS

CHIEF AGILITY OFFICER
FOUNDER

Peter B. Stevens is an Executive, Coach, Author, and Certified Scrum Trainer. He most recently served as Chief Agility Officer at Vivior AG, the Swiss digital health startup, and is co-founder of Agile-Executives.org, Personal Agility Institute, and World Agility Forum. He is an instrument-rated pilot, speaks 4 languages, and lives in Zurich, Switzerland with his family and 3 cats.

MARIA MATARELLI

FOUNDER & CEO
FORMULA INK

Maria Matarelli is an Executive Agile Coach, Consultant to the Fortune 100, and an international best-selling author. Maria and her team consult businesses to reach breakthrough results by applying Agile methodologies from startups reaching $35 Million-dollar valuations to streamlining Millions in cost savings for Billion-dollar organizations. Maria is the founder and President of Formula Ink and co-founder of the Agile Marketing Academy and Personal Agility Institute.